정신장애인의
인권 향상을 위한 지침

Guidelines for the Promotion of
Human Rights of Persons with Mental Disorders

국립중앙도서관 출판시도서목록(CIP)

정신장애인의 인권 향상을 위한 지침 / 지은이: 세계보건기구 정신보
건 및 약물남용예방 분과 ; 옮긴이: 신영전, 최영은. -- 파주: 한울,
2007   p. ;   cm. -- (한울아카데미 ; 962)
권말부록으로 "인권 관련 국제 선언문", " '정신장애인의 인권 향상
을 위한 지침' 및 인권 관련 국제 선언문의 영문본" 수록
원서명: Guidelines for the promotion of human rights of persons
with mental disorders
원저자명: Division of Mental Health and Prevention of Substance
Abuse, World Health Organization
ISBN   978-89-460-3768-7 93330
338.3-KDC4
362.2-DDC21   CIP2007002274

정신장애인의
인권 향상을 위한
지침

세계보건기구 정신보건 및 약물남용예방 분과 지음

신영전·최영은 옮김

Guidelines for the Promotion of
Human Rights of Persons with Mental Disorders

한울
아카데미

Guidelines for the Promotion
of Human Rights of Persons with Mental Disorders

Published by the World Health Organization in 1996
under the title *Guidelines for the Promotion*
of Human Rights of Persons with Mental Disorders
ⓒ World Health Organization 1996

인권의 '바로미터(barometer)', 정신장애인 인권

아마 언젠가는 정신장애인이 동일 국가의 다른 시민들과 정확하게 동일
한 권리를 가져야만 하고, 근본적으로 그들이 선택하고 결정한 삶을 살
권리를 가져야 한다는 것을 인정하게 될 것이다.

— 주디 체임벌린(Judi Chamberlin)

민주화 이후 한국 사회에서 인권이 빠르게 신장되고 있다. 비록 아직
도 산적한 과제가 많기는 하지만, 최근에 보이는 인권 신장의 '빠른 속도'
는 분명 특별한 것이다. 1997년 국가인권위원회 설립이 그러한 변화의
가시적인 증거 중 하나이고, 「성매매방지 및 피해자보호 등에 관한 법률」
제정이나 '호주제 폐지' 의결 등은 그것의 조기 실현 가능성을 의심했던
많은 이들에게 큰 충격을 줄 만큼 전격적인 것이었다. 이러한 자신감을
바탕으로 2004년 9월에는 전 세계 인권운동가들을 서울로 불러 모아
인권을 논하는 '세계국가인권기구대회'를 유치하기도 했다. 또한 최근
에는 「장애인차별금지 및 권리구제 등에 관한 법률」이 제정되기도 했다.
이제 우리는 학교나 직장, 그리고 정책의 결정과 시행 과정에서 '인권'을
이야기하는 것이 자연스러운 일이 된, 이른바 '인권의 시대'에 살게 된

것 같다.

하지만 문제는 이러한 인권의 증진이 모든 이들에게 고루 이루어지고 있지 않다는 것이다. 2004년 11월에 국가인권위원회 주최로 열린 '정신과 시설 인권 현장 공청회'에서 발표된 조사 결과에 따르면, 정신질환자들에 대한 강제 입원이 여전히 많이 이루어지고 있고, 이들은 열악한 수용 시설에서 반인권적인 격리와 강박 등에 시달리고 있다고 한다. 법정 시설에 입소한 이들이 이러할진대, 만 명이 훨씬 넘을 것으로 추정되는 비인가 불법 시설에 수용되어 있는 이들의 인권 실태는 오죽할 것인가? 1983년 모 방송국에서 정신질환자의 참혹한 실태가 보도된 후, 「정신보건법」이 제정되고 정부 내 주무 부처도 생겨났으며, 최근에는 지역사회 정신보건 관련 사업들이 늘어나는 등 일부 긍정적인 변화가 나타나고 있다. 그럼에도 불구하고 정신장애인의 인권은 여전히 '원시적인' 수준을 벗어나지 못하고 있으며, 더욱이 최근에는 관련 논의조차 완고한 제도의 뒤편으로 밀려나고 있는 인상이다.

세계 도처의 인권운동가들이 모여 인류 모두가 예외 없이 마땅히 누려야 할 인권의 가치에 대해 뜨겁게 토론하고 있던 그 시간, 다른 한편에서는 여전히 불법 강제 구금이 성행하고 있었다. 서울에서 차로 30분만 달리면 되는 곳에 위치한 비인가 시설에 불법으로 집단 감금되어 전문가의 진단이나 치료도 받지 못한 채 종일 침대에 묶여 있는 이들을 만날 수 있었던 것이다. '선진 한국' 인권의 이러한 '양극화' 현상을 우리는 어떻게 설명해야 할까?

인권에는 경계가 없다. '부자의 인권'이 따로 있고 '가난한 이들의 인권'이 따로 있는 것이 아니다. 그러기에 오늘날 한국 사회에서 나타나는 이 '인권의 양극화'는 그 자체가 '반인권적'이다. 그리고 그 반인권의 중심에 바로 정신질환자들의 고통이 있다.

"모든 인간은 태어날 때부터 자유로우며 그 존엄성과 권리는 동등하다. 인간은 천부적으로 이성과 양심을 부여받았으며 서로 형제애의 정신으로 행동해야 한다." 이러한 세계인권선언은 비단 정신장애인에게 국한된 이야기가 아니다. 그러나 정신장애인의 인권은 몇 가지 이유에서 특별한 의미를 가진다. 첫째, 정신장애인은 다른 집단에 비해 인권을 침해받을 가능성이 매우 높은 이들이다. 둘째, 정신장애인에게 인권은 차별, 낙인, 배제 등으로부터 이들을 지켜주는 거의 유일한 수단이다. 더 나아가 정신질환자의 삶의 질을 보장하는 체계를 만들어내기 위한 새로운 시도에 인권은 핵심적인 또는 거의 유일한 동력을 제공한다. 마지막으로, 정신장애인의 인권은 달성하기 어려운 만큼 한 사회의 인권 수준이 진정 얼마나 성숙했는지를 가늠할 수 있는 인권의 '바로미터' 기능을 수행한다.

최근 정신장애인의 인권을 보호하기 위한 취지로 「정신보건법」의 개정 작업이 진행 중이다. 이러한 법 개정 과정은 고스틴(L. O. Gostin)이 분류한 정신장애 관련 네 가지 권리, 즉 자유권, 존엄권, 평등권, 법적 권리를 보장하기 위한 제도적 장치들이 마련되는 기회가 되어야 한다. 하지만 상황은 절박한 반면 갈 길은 너무 멀어 보인다.

현재까지 정신장애인의 인권에 관한 규정은 1991년 12월 국제연합(United Nations: UN) 총회에서 결의된 「정신장애인 보호와 정신보건 의료 향상을 위한 원칙(Principles for the Protection of Persons with Mental Illness and for the Improvement of Mental Health Care, 이하 MI 원칙)」에 기초하고 있다. 이 책은 바로 이 MI 원칙의 실제 적용을 위해 세계보건기구(World Health Organization: WHO)가 만든 지침서이다. 오랜 시간이 지나기는 했지만 이 MI 원칙은 여전히 전 세계에서 정신장애인 인권의 기본적인 원칙과 지침으로 사용되고 있다. 따라서 당연히 한국 사회에도 이 원칙과 지침을 일찍 번역해 정신장애인의 인권 보호 정책과 활동에 활용했어야 했다. 뒤늦게나마 이 책을 번역해 소개하게 된 것을 기쁘게 생각한다.

세계보건기구가 만든 지침서에 추가해 책 말미에는 정신장애인의 인권에 관련된 각종 선언을 모았다. 또한 번역의 한계를 보완하기 위해 책 뒤에 영문본을 함께 실었다.

이 번역본이 나오는 데 국가인권위원회의 지원이 큰 도움이 되었다. 한양의대 예방의학교실 연구원들도 교정 과정에 참여해 도움을 주었다. 특별히 남희경 연구원의 수고가 각별했다. 아울러 도서출판 한울의 흔쾌한 출판 동의와 꼼꼼한 교정은 이 책의 완성도를 높이는 데 큰 도움이 되었다.

부디 이 책이 이 시간에도 정신장애인의 인권 보호를 위해 시설과 거리에서 땀 흘리고 있는 인권 단체 활동가, 국가인권위원회 관계자, 시설 종사자, 자원봉사자, 그리고 특별히 정신장애에 대한 편견을 극복하고 스스로의 인권을 지키기 위해 노력하고 있는 정신장애인과 가족들에게 조금이라도 도움이 되기를 바란다. 우리 사회 정신장애인 인권에 진전이 이루어진다면 전적으로 이들의 노력 덕분이기에 역자들은 이 책으로 발생하는 수익이 있다면 전액을 정신장애인 인권을 위해 애쓰는 분들에게 기부하기로 약속했다.

2007년 7월
신영전

차례

정신장애인의 인권 향상을 위한 지침

이 지침은 1991년 UN 이사회에서 채택한 결의문 등 정신보건
분야의 국제적인 주요 문헌에 따라 정신장애인의 인권 존중의
증진 및 평가와 정신보건 의료 향상에 관한 도구들을 담고 있다.

핵심 단어: 인권, 정신장애, 정신장애인, 정신보건법

세계보건기구
정신보건 및 약물남용예방 분과
정신장애 관리
(제네바, 1996)

논의를 시작하며

세계보건기구(WHO)의 '정신장애인 지원 사업단(Initiative of Support to People Disabled by Mental Illness)'은 정신장애의 치료와 예방에 관한 WHO 의 작업 중 하나이다. 이는 만성 정신장애인을 위한 지역사회의 양질의 서비스와 이 분야의 새로운 발전에 대한 정보를 전문가와 정부에게 제공하는 데 박차를 가하기 위한 시도이다. 이 사업단은 만성 정신 질환 의 장애 영향을 감소시키는 것을 돕고, 만성 정신장애에 대한 낙인에 더해져 치료와 재활의 노력을 방해하는 사회적·환경적 장벽을 명확히 보여주는 것을 목적으로 한다. 또한 정신보건 서비스의 기획·제공·평가 에 관련된 것들과 소비자의 권한을 강화하고자 한다.

다음의 기관은 공식적으로 이러한 시도에 함께하고 관련된 다양한 활동에 참여했다.

- The Queensland Northern Penninsula and Mackay Region Mental Health Service(centred in Townsville, Australia)
- British Columbia Ministry of Health — Mental Health Services(Vancouver, Canada)
- Centro Studi e Ricerche Salute Mentale — Regione Autonoma Friuli Venezia-Giulia, Trieste(Italy)
- Highland Health Board — Mental Health Unit and Highland Regional Council(Inverness, Scotland, UK)
- SOGG(Rotterdam) / Ministry of Health(The Netherlands)

The Dowaki Chiba Hospital(Funabashi, Japan) 또한 일부 활동에 참여했으며, 다른 기관들도 이 활동에 참여하는 것에 대해 다양한 수준에서 논의 중이다.

이에 관한 추가 정보는 아래에 요청할 수 있다.

Dr. J. M. Bertolote
Mental Disorders Control
WHO — Division of Mental Health and Prevention of Substance Abuse
1211 Geneva-27 Switzerland

정신장애인 지원 사업단

Initiative of Support to People Disabled by Mental Illness

자문 네트워크

P. Alterwain, Uruguay	G. Long, Canada
L. Bachrach, USA	V. Nagaswami, India
P. Barham, UK	D. Peck, UK
V. Basauri, Spain	A. Pitta, Brazil
J. Chamberlin, USA	T. Powell, USA
P. Chanoit, France	H. Richards, UK
F. Costa, Sweden	F. Rotelli, Italy
M. Farkas, USA	B. Saraceno, Italy
G. Harnois, Canada	K. Schilder, The Netherlands
T. Held, Germany	G. Scribner, Canada
B. James, Australia	T. Takizawa, Japan
M. Jansen, USA	H. Wagenborg, The Netherlands
L. Lara Palma, Spain	R. Warner, USA

감사의 글

이 지침의 초안은 다음에 제시된 많은 전문가들의 지원과 조언을 받았
는데 예상했던 대로 그들이 대표하는 넓은 범위의 이해에 따라 전문가들
의 견해는 매우 다양했다. 주요한 상이점에 대한 간략한 검토는 다음의
'들어가는 말' 부분에서 제시했다. 전문가들은 물론이고 그들이 대표하
는 일부 NGO에서 제공하는 지원에 대해서도 깊이 감사한다.

Dr. E. M. Sommer, Mrs. E. Fuller, Mr. S. Poitras는 지침의 제작에 도움을
주었다. Dr. J. Orley와 Dr. S. Flache는 지속적인 격려로 힘이 되어주었으며,
통찰력 있는 비평을 제공했다. Mrs. T. Drouillet와 Mrs. N. Hurst는 이
문서의 여러 버전을 타이핑하고 재타이핑하는 노고를 끝까지 감수했다.

J. E. Arboleda-Florez
WHO Collaborating Centre for Research
Calgary, Alb, Canada
Training in Mental Health
Calgary, Alb, Canada

P. Barham
Hamlet Trust
London, UK

A. Carmi
World Association for Medical Law
Haifa, Israel

J. Chamberlin
Center for Psychiatric Rehabilitation,
Boston University
Boston, MA, USA

P. S. Cohen(故)
International Commission of Jurists
Chene-Bougeries, Switzerland

W. J. Curran
WHO Collaborating Centre for Health
Legislation, Harvard School of Public
Health
Boston, MA, USA

G. Harnois
WHO Collaborating Centre for Research
and Training in Mental Health
Verdun, Que, Canada

E. Heim
International Federation of Psychotherapy
Bern, Switzerland

J. H. Henderson
Consultant in Mental Health
Weston Favell, Northampton, UK

A. Kraut
Buenos Aires, Argentina

C. Louzoun
European Committee on Law, Ethics and Psychiatry
Paris, France

N. Macdermot
International Commission of Jurists
Chene-Bougeries, Switzerland

M. O'Hagan
World Federation of Psychiatric Users
Auckland, New Zealand

K. Pawlik
International Union of Psychological Science
Hamburg, Germany

L. Eisenberg
Department of Social Medicine and Health Policy, Harvard Medical School
Boston, MA, USA

G. Elvy
Canberra, Australia

C. Gendreau
Centre de Recherche en Droit Public Universite de Montreal
Montreal, Canada

M. G. Giannichedda
Centro Franco Basaglia
Rome, Italy

L. O. Gostin
Georgetown/Johns Hopkins Program on Law and Public Health
Washington, D.C., USA

T. Harding
Institut Universitaire de Médecine Légale
Geneva, Switzerland

N. Sartorius
World Psychiatric Association
Geneva, Switzerland

H. Sell
Regional Advisor for Health & Behaviour, WHO Regional Office for South East Asia
New Delhi, India

E. Sorel
World Association for Social Psychiatry
Washington, D.C., USA

A. Szokoloczy-Grobet
Association Psychiatrie, Responsabilite et Societe / Les Sans Voix
Geneva, Switzerland

J. G. V. Taborda
WHO Collaborating Centre for Research and Training in Mental Health
Porto Alegre, Brazil

F. Torres Gonzalez
Mental Health Area, Granada University Hospital
Granada, Spain

W. van den Graaf
Clientunion
Amsterdam, The Netherlands

들어가는 말

정신장애인의 가장 기본적인 권리만이라도 지원하는 국제적 도구가 생기기까지는 오랜 시간이 걸렸다. 1991년 12월 17일 국제연합(United Nations: UN) 이사회는 결의문 46/119를 통해 '정신장애인 보호와 정신보건 의료 향상을 위한 원칙'을 채택했다. 이는 1978년 UN 인권위원회가 정신장애로 인해 억류된 사람들을 보호하는 문제를 연구하기 위해 산하위원회에 소수자 보호와 차별 예방을 요구하여 시작된 14년 작업의 결실이다. 이 결의문의 초안은 10년 이상 경제사회이사회에서 논의·토론한 끝에 마침내 완성되었다.

이 원칙의 최종 구성과 범위(25개 원칙의 일부는 매우 상세하다)는 타질병 또는 장애와 관련된 이전의 UN 결의문과는 약간 다르게 제작되었다. 이 결의문에 어떻게 생명을 불어넣을 것인지가 지침 제작 과정에서 중요한 이슈였다. 그렇게 하지 않으면 이러한 훌륭한 문서에 있는 인권에 대한 관심이 응급실, 병동, 외래 치료 센터, 법정, 교도소와 같이 인권이 다루어지는 곳에서 적용되기가 어려울 것이다. 원칙의 이해와 실행을 촉진하는 부가적인 도구가 필요해졌고, 세계보건기구가 이 도구의 제공을 총괄해야 한다는 보편적인 합의가 있었다. 전문가들, 비정부기구(NGO)와 협의한 후, 지침을 명백히 하기 위해 사용자가 쉽게 이해할 수 있는 질문의 형태로 지침을 제작하기로 결정했다.

세계보건기구의 정신보건 및 약물남용예방 분과가 다음에 나오는 지침을 제작했으며, 이로써 서명자들은 결의문 46/119를 실제로 적용할 수 있게 될 것이다. 이 지침은 결의문 46/119의 여러 하부 항목만 아니라 주요 원칙들 하나하나와 관련된 상황을 심층 평가하기 위해 만들어졌다. 전통적인 시민권 및 참정권 외에도 적절한 정신건강 치료에 관한 권리가 이 결의문 46/119에 포함되었다. 또 이 지침은 정책 결정자와 정신보건 의료 제공자들이 지역사회나 국가 차원의 정신보건 의료 사업을 평가할 때 이에 대한 기준을 제시하기 위한 기본적인 질 보증(quality assurance) 이슈들을 다룬다.

또한 국가와 지역적인 수준에서 정신장애 인권 수준에 대해 매우 간단하고 보편적인 평가를 제공하기 위해 지침에서 도출된 간명한 점검표를 제작했다. 점검표의 주요 목적은 더욱 심층적인 지침을 위한 동반 도구(companion tool)로서 상황에 대해 민감하게 평가할 수 있도록 하는 것이다.

이를 위해 이 문서는 세 가지 주요한 영역으로 구성되었다. 1부는 지침의 전문(全文)이고 2부는 점검표이며, 부록으로는 ① 지침 제작에 관여한 협력자의 목록, ② 보편적으로 정신보건 분야와 관련된 일부 엄선된 UN 선언문과 결의문 등이 포함되어 있다.

1부의 지침(UN 결의문 원칙 중 중요한 본문을 포함하기로 했다)은 각각의 원칙이 적용되는 범위를 확인하려는 이들을 안내하기 위해 의도된 일련의 질문들이 뒤따른다. 정확하고 일정한 또는 옳거나 그른 응답을 가진 척도는 아니며, 지역적 특성과 전통 및 자원 등에 대한 여지를 고려하여 주로 각각의 원칙을 모니터링하는 대안적인 접근을 제공하기 위해 의도된 질적 도구이다.

이러한 질문들은 원칙의 실제 사실이 무엇인지를 설명하려는 의미이지, 그것을 속속들이 규명해내려는 목적은 아니다. 오히려 고찰하고 검토하기 위한 항목의 예를 부각시키기 위한 취지이다. 문화, 개발 수준, 법적 전통, 정치적·종교적 체제 등과 같은 요인의 다양성에 좌우되기 때문에 모든 질문들이 적용되거나 모든 지역에 관련되는 것은 아니라는 점에 주의하는 것이 중요하다.

그러나 단순히 실행을 위한 결의문 및 지침이 존재하는 것만으로 이것이 반드시 사람들에게 유익하다고 보장할 수는 없다. 대부분의 경우 일부 공식적인 기관(예를 들어 의회, 보건복지부, 의료심의회)이 이 원칙을 비준하거나 국가 수준에서 공식적으로 이를 채택한다. 다음으로 이의 실시를 검증하는 작업이 뒤따르는데 정신보건 및 인권과 관련된 일부 NGO들은 이를 실행하기에 적합한 기관이다.

정신보건 법률과 법률의 실행은 사회 발전에 매우 중요하다. 1993년 세계은행에서 발표한 「세계개발보고서(World Development Report)」에 따르면 DALY(Disability-adjusted life years, 장애보정생존연수)라는 지표로 측정되는 정신 질환이 경제와 공중 보건에 주는 부담과 정신장애 및 관련 질환에 드는 비용은 사회개발 과정에 큰 걸림돌이 되는 것으로 나타났다.

나아가 법 규정을 고수하는 것은 예측 가능하고 성문화된 규범과 제도를 제시한다는 의미에서 사회 발전에 중요하다. 법 규정의 고수는 그 자체로 사회의 안정적인 힘이다. 정신보건 법률은 바로 취약 인구 계층에 초점이 맞춰져 있기 때문에 법 규정을 제정하거나 강화하는 데 중요한 첫걸음이 되며 사회 발전을 촉진한다.

이 문헌을 준비하는 과정에 많은 사람들이 참여했다. 일부 전문가들은 UN 결의문 최종 원문에 불만을 표시했고, 향후 지침의 실행과 모니터링을 보장하는 것에도 불만을 표시했다.

일반적으로 정신장애인의 권익을 대표하는 이러한 전문가들의 관점은 보건 정책과 관련해 강제적인 규범이 적용되는 국가들의 권리와 대립하여 시민권 및 참정권의 중요성에 대한 몇십 년간의 오랜 논쟁을 반영하고 있다.

그들의 관점에서 볼 때, UN 결의문은 '치료의 권리'가 아닌 '인간의 기본권'에 집중되었어야 한다. (특히 Daes Report에서 Pally Report로 변경되고 Steel Report로 이어져 사용하고 있는) 소수자 보호와 차별 금지에 관한 위원회에서의 토론 과정에서 치료에 관한 이슈의 내용들은 그들의 관점에서는 여전히 그것의 본래 의도를 왜곡하고, 영역을 확장하며, 정신장애인의 권익을 약화시키고 있다. 이러한 문제 제기를 받아들이지 않고 있기는 하지만, UN 결의문은 시민권, 참정권, 사회적·경제적·문화적 권리 모든 면에서 향후 주요한 국제적 조치를 설명한다. 그 자체만으로도 아래와 같은 체임벌린(J. Chamberlin)의 말을 마음에 되새기며 보급되고 촉진되기 위한 적절한 수단이 될 만한 가치가 충분하다.

아마 언젠가는 정신장애인이 동일 국가의 다른 시민들과 정확하게 동일한 권리를 가져야만 하고, 근본적으로 그들이 선택하고 결정한 삶을 살 권리를 가져야 한다는 것을 인정하게 될 것이다.

이 문서는 위에 언급된 조항이 납득되고 각 지역의 언어로 널리 이용될 때 비로소 유용할 수 있다. 그러므로 권익 단체들은 각 지역의 언어로 번역을 장려하고 어떻게든 적용시키도록 노력해야 한다. 정신보건 및 약물남용예방 분과는 각 지역판의 출판에 대해 감사하며, 이는 널리 확대되어야 할 것이다.

세계보건기구

정신보건 및 약물남용예방 분과

정신장애 관리

(스위스 제네바)

제1부

'정신장애인 보호와 정신보건 의료
향상을 위한 원칙'과 적용을 위한 지침

Guidelines for the Application
of the Principles for the Protection of Persons
with Mental Illness and the Improvement of Mental Health Care

정신장애인 보호와 정신보건 의료 향상을 위한 원칙

Principles for the Protection of Persons with Mental Illness and the Improvement of Mental Health Care

1991년 12월 17일 국제연합 총회 46/119 결의문으로 채택

이 UN 원칙은 장애, 인종, 피부색, 성별, 언어, 종교, 정치적 입장 또는 기타 견해, 국가나 민족 혹은 사회적 출신, 법적·사회적 지위, 연령, 재산 또는 출생 에 근거를 둔 어떠한 종류의 차별 없이 적용되어야 한다.

정의 definition

이 원칙에서,

(a) '대리인(counsel)'은 법적으로 혹은 기타 자격을 갖춘 대리인을 지칭한다.

(b) '독립적인 권한 기관(independent authority)'은 국내법 규정에 의해 권한이 부여된 독립적인 기관을 의미한다.

(c) '정신보건 의료'는 개인의 정신 건강 상태의 분석 및 진단, 정신 질환이나 정신장애로 추정되는 질환에 대한 치료, 의료 및 재활을 포함한다.

(d) '정신보건 시설'은 정신보건 의료 제공을 주된 기능으로 하는 모든 시설 또는 시설의 단위를 의미한다.

(e) '정신보건 전문가'는 의사, 심리치료사, 간호사, 사회복지사 또는 기타 정신보건에 유용한 특수한 기술을 가진 이로서, 적합한 훈련을 거쳐 자격을 갖춘 종사자들을 의미한다.

(f) '환자'는 정신보건 의료를 제공받는 사람으로서, 정신보건 시설에 수용되어 있는 모든 사람은 여기에 포함된다.

(g) '개인 대리인(personal representative)'은 법에 의해 어떠한 특정 측면에서 환자의 이익을 대변하는 사람 또는 환자를 대신해 특정 권리를 행사할 의무를 지니도록 지정된 사람을 의미하며, 국내법에 의해 달리 지정되지 않은 경우 미성년자의 부모 또는 법적 후견인도 이에 포함된다.

(h) '심사 기관'은 정신보건 시설에 비자발적으로 수용되어 있는 환자를 심사하기 위해 원칙 17에 따라 설립된 단체를 의미한다.

1. 이 정의를 따르도록 하는 현행 법률 기관에서는 이 내용(또는 동등한 관점)에 대해 어떻게 정의하고 있는가?

2. 만약 앞의 정의와 현행 법률 기관의 정의 간에 차이가 존재한다면 법률 기관은,

   a. 환자의 권리를 원칙보다 더 강하게 보호하는가, 또는 더 약하게 보호하는가?

   b. 원칙보다 정신보건 의료의 향상에 더 많이 초점을 맞추는가, 또는 그렇지 않은가?

일반적인 제한 사항 general limitation clause

이 원칙에 규정된 권리의 행사는 해당인 또는 타인의 건강이나 안전을 보호하기 위해, 또는 공공의 안전, 질서, 건강 또는 도덕, 타인의 기본권과 자유를 보호하기 위해 필요한 것으로서 법으로 규정되어 있는 사항에 의해서만 제한될 수 있다.

1. 이 원칙에 열거되어 있는 권리를 행사할 때 제한을 받는가? 만약 그렇다면 어느 원칙이며 어느 범위까지인가?

2. 원칙에 열거되어 있는 권리를 행사할 때 법에 의해서만 제한을 받는가? 그렇지 않다면 그 제한은 어떻게 규정되는가? 그 제한은 사전에 지정되는가? 대중에게 알려져 있는가?

3. 원칙에 열거되어 있는 권리의 행사는 해당인 또는 타인의 건강과 안전을 보호하기 위해서 필요한 경우에만 제한되는가?

4. 원칙에 열거되어 있는 권리의 행사는 공공의 안전, 질서, 건강 또는 도덕, 타인의 기본권과 자유를 보호하기 위해서만 제한되는가?

5. 다음 중 알려진 것이 있다면, 이 원칙에 열거되어 있는 권리를 제한할 수 있는 특정한 근거는 무엇인가?
   a. 해당인의 건강과 안전을 보호하기 위해
   b. 타인의 건강과 안전을 보호하기 위해
   c. 공공의 안전을 보호하기 위해

d. 공공의 질서를 보호하기 위해

e. 공공의 건강을 보호하기 위해

f. 공공의 도덕을 지키기 위해

g. 타인의 기본권과 자유를 보호하기 위해

근본적 자유와 기본권
fundamental freedoms and basic rights

1. 모든 사람은 보건의료 및 사회적 보호 제도 안에서 가장 적절한 정신보건 의료를 제공받을 권리가 있다.

1.1. 모든 사람은 가장 적절한 정신보건 의료를 제공받을 권리를 가지고 있는가? 어떠한 정신보건 의료가 가능하며 누구에게 가능한가? 해당 국가의 모든 대상 지역에서 정신보건 의료를 제공하는가? 모든 대상 지역은 적절하게 재정 지원을 받는가?

1.2. 보건의료 체계 내에서 정신보건의 중요성이 어떻게 강조되는가? 일반적인 보건 서비스에서 재원 조달 또는 제3자에 의한 지불 보상이 치료에 제한을 가하는 경우가 많은데, 정신보건에서 이러한 문제가 생기지 않도록 어떻게 재정을 운영하는가?

1.3. 정신보건 서비스, 사회보장 서비스, 일반 보건 서비스는 어떤 방식으로 연계 또는 통합되어 있는가? 이들은 근접해 있는가? 그렇다면 얼마나 근접해 있는가? 근접해 있지 않다면 이들 간의 연계 방법이 제공되어 있는가? 이들은 전자 통신으로 연계되어 있는가? 그렇지 않다면 이들 간에 (다른 형태의) 통신이 가능한가?

1.4. 보건의료 시설에는 사회복지 부서가 있는가? 없다면 정신보건 시설, 일반 보건 시설 및 기타 시설과 상호 협력하여 합의를 이끌어낼 수 있는 다른 부서가 있는가?

1.5. (치료 전, 치료 중, 치료 후에) 정신장애인의 지원을 위한 어떤 복지

사업이 있는가?

1.6. 다음 사항에 대해 다양한 인구 집단 간의 차이 또는 지리적인 차이는 어떠한가?

- 정신보건 의료의 접근성 (예를 들어, 시골 또는 도시에서부터 정신보건 의료 시설까지의 평균 접근 시간)
- 정신보건 의료 시설의 직원/환자 비율

1.7. 정해진 지리적 구역 내에서, 다른 유형의 보건의료 시설의 직원/환자 비율에 대비하여 정신보건 의료 시설의 직원/환자 비율은 어떠한가?

1.8. 도보로 한 시간 거리 내에서 어떤 신경정신과 약제를 얻을 수 있는가? (원칙 10 참조)

2. 모든 정신장애인 또는 정신장애로 치료를 받고 있는 사람은 인간으로서 고유한 존엄성을 토대로 한 인류애와 존경을 바탕으로 치료받아야 한다.

2.1. 모든 정신장애인은 그들의 존엄성을 토대로 인류애와 존경을 바탕으로 치료받고 있는가?

2.2. 이를 보장하는 법률이 있는가?

2.3. 정신보건 의료를 제공하는 다양한 분야의 전문 단체에 의해 채택된 도덕 지침이 있는가? 이러한 도덕 지침을 따르지 않을 경우 그 결과는 어떠한가?

2.4. 모든 정신장애인은 적절한 시기에 그들의 권리를 그들이 이해할 수 있는 형식이나 언어로 고지받는가?

3. 모든 정신장애인 또는 정신장애 치료를 받고 있는 사람은 경제적·성적

착취 및 기타 유형의 착취, 신체적 학대를 비롯한 여러 가지 학대, 치료를 저해하는 행위로부터 보호받을 권리가 있다.

3.1. 정신장애인이 신체적·성적·경제적으로 또는 기타 방식으로 착취 당하는가? 반대로, 그러한 학대로부터 어떻게 보호받는가?

3.2. 그러한 착취나 학대를 금지할 법률이 있는가? 그러한 형태의 착취나 학대에 대한 민사상·형사상·행정상의 처벌이 있는가? 그러한 착취에 대한 형사상 처벌이 더 엄중한가? 즉, 일반적으로 소수자에 대한 형사상 처벌보다 '보호 계층'인 정신장애인의 착취 및 학대에 대한 처벌이 더 엄중한가?

3.3. 잠재적인 장래의 고용주가 착취 또는 학대 범죄에 관한 정보에 접근할 수 있는 것과 같이, 보호 계층 일원에 대한 착취나 학대를 포함한 범죄가 입증되는 사람들에 관한 기록이 공적으로 활용 가능한가?(원칙 22 참조)

4. 정신장애를 근거로 한 차별이 있어서는 안 된다. '차별'은 기본권의 동등한 향유를 저해하는 모든 분류, 배제 또는 선호를 의미한다. 정신장애인의 권리를 보호하거나 이들의 치료를 위한 특별한 조치들은 차별이라고 보지 않는다. 정신장애인 또는 다른 개인의 인권을 보호하기 위해 필요한 것으로 이 원칙에 따라 행해진 분류, 배제, 선호 등은 차별이라고 보지 않는다.

4.1. 정신장애인을 대상으로 한 차별(예를 들면 취업, 공공 서비스나 오락 시설에 대한 접근, 형사재판 체계)의 증거가 있는가?

4.2. 이러한 차별을 금지하는 법률이 있는가? 그렇다면 그러한 법률은 시행되고 있는가?

4.3. 예를 들어, 원하지 않는 치료로부터의 자유 또는 아래 원칙 1의 5항에서 논의된 사적인 권리와 같이, 사회의 다른 구성원에게는 존재하지 않는 법률적이거나 실제적인 권리에 대한 제약이 정신장애인에게 있는가?

4.4. 그러한 판단이 내려질 수 있는 방법은 무엇인가? 예를 들어,

  a. 노동을 강요받는가?

  b. 이러한 노동자들이 비정신장애인 노동자와 동일한 보수를 받고 있는가?

  c. 보수는 어떤 방식인가? 즉, 환자들이 보수를 받는 데 기본적인 권리를 보장받는가? 치료 시설에서 감금 상태에 처해 있어도 변제가 가능한가? 처벌에서 자유로운가? 요컨대 환자들은 무보수 노동을 강요받는가?

  d. 환자들이 보수를 받는다고 가정할 때, 환자들은 그 지역의 화폐로 직접 보수를 지급받는가? 단순히 보관을 위해 다른 누군가에게 지급되는가?

4.5. 정신장애인을 위한 우호적 실행 프로그램이 있는가?

5. 모든 정신장애인은 「세계인권선언」, 「경제적·사회적·문화적 권리에 관한 국제 협약」, 「시민권 및 정치적 권리에 관한 국제 협약」은 물론이고, 기타 「장애인 권리선언」이나 「모든 형태의 억류·구금하에 있는 사람들을 보호하기 위한 원칙」 등 관련 협정에서 인정하는 사회적·정치적·경제적·문화적 권리를 행사할 권리를 가져야 한다.

5.1. 정신장애인은 다음과 같은 시민권 및 참정권과 경제적·사회적·문화적 권리를 행사할 수 있는가?

a. 결혼할 권리

b. 재산권

c. 사상, 의식 및 종교의 자유를 가질 권리

d. 투표권

e. 사상과 표현의 자유를 가질 권리

f. 노동, 취업 선택의 자유, 적절한 작업 조건, 그리고 실업에 대해
   보호를 받을 권리

g. 교육의 권리 (원칙 2 '미성년자에 대한 보호' 참조)

h. 자녀를 가지며 양육할 수 있는 권리

i. 이주 및 주거 선택의 권리 (개인이 원한다고 가정할 때)

j. 그들의 권리를 보호하기 위해 적당한 법적인 도움을 받을 수 있
   는 권리와 특정한 합법적 절차를 밟아 그들의 상태를 충분히 고
   려받을 수 있는 권리[1]

k. 개인의 의료 기록을 열람할 수 있는 권리 (원칙 19 참조)

l. 잔인하고 비인간적이거나 낮은 수준의 치료 또는 처벌로부터 자
   유로울 권리 (부록의 「장애인 권리선언」 참조)

6. 정신장애로 인한 법적 행위무능력자 판정과 그에 따라 개인 대리인을 선임
해야 한다는 판단은, 국내법에 의해 설립된 독립적이고 공정한 심사 기관에서
공정한 심리를 거친 후에 내려야만 한다. 법적 행위능력 여부를 판정받는
대상자에게는 대리인을 선임할 권리가 주어져야 한다. 만약 법적 행위능력
판정 대상자가 대리인을 스스로 구하지 않은 경우, 대리인 선임에 필요한
지불 능력이 없다면 무료로 대리인이 지정되어야 한다. 이때 대리인은 동일

---

1) 부록의 UN, 「장애인 권리선언」(1975), 원칙 11 참조.

사건에서 정신보건 시설 또는 그 직원을 대리할 수 없으며, 또한 가족 간 이익의 충돌이 없다는 법원의 결정이 없는 이상은 해당 능력 판정 대상자의 가족원을 동시에 대리할 수 없다. 법적 행위능력과 개인 대리인 필요성에 대한 결정은 국내법에 지정된 바와 같이 합당한 기간을 두고 재심되어야 한다. 법적 행위능력 판정 대상이 되는 정신장애인과 그 정신장애인의 대리인 및 다른 이해관계인에게는 결정 사항에 대해 상급법원에 항소할 수 있는 권리가 주어져야 한다.

6.1. 국가의 법률 체계 내에서 법적 행위능력 또는 무능력에 관한 개념은 무엇인가?

6.2. 그 개념은 어떻게 한정되는가?

  a. 어떤 것에 대한 행위무능력인가?

    ⅰ. 법정에 출두하는 것?

    ⅱ. 의지를 기술하는 것?

    ⅲ. 계약을 맺는 것?

    ⅳ. 정보공개에 대한 승낙, 실험적 치료 또는 임상 시험을 포함한 치료에 대한 의사를 결정하는 것?

  b. 그 기간은?

    ⅰ. 행위능력의 회복을 위한 조항이나 절차가 있는가?

    ⅱ. 그 사안은 자동적으로 재고되는가? 만약 그렇다면 얼마나 자주 재고되는가? 요청에 의해 재고되는가? 그렇다면 누구의 요청에 의해서인가?

6.3. 개인의 법적 행위능력에 대한 판단 절차는 어떠한가?

6.4. 개인의 법적 행위능력이 결여되었다고 판단할 때 파생되는 결과는 무엇인가?

6.5. 행위능력의 심리에 대리인이 필요한가? 누가 그러한 대리인을 결정하는가?

6.6. 개인에게 대리인 지정을 위한 지불 수단이 부족한 경우 어떠한 조치가 취해지는가?

6.7. 환자의 대리인이 다른 이익 단체도 대리하는가? 예를 들면, 정신보건 의료 시설(또는 그곳 직원) 또는 환자 가족을 대리하는가?

6.8. 누가 이익의 충돌에 관한 경우를 판단하는가? 이러한 판단 결정에 기준을 적용하는가? 그렇다면 어떠한 기준을 적용하는가?

6.9. 개인은 이의를 제기할 권리를 가지는가? 그렇다면 이의 제기의 순서는? 이의는 동일한 기관에 제기되는가? 또는 상급 기관에 제기되는가? 이의 제기는 실질적 또는 절차상의 문제, 또는 두 가지 모두에 기초하여 받아들여지는가?

6.10. 타인도 이의 제기의 권리를 가지는가? 그렇다면 어떤 사람이 그러한 권리를 가지는가?(예를 들어 치료 시설, 친척, 상속인, 대리인이나 후견인, 미성년자를 대신해 의지를 이행하는 자 등 다양한 가능성이 포함될 수 있다.)

7. 법원이나 기타 담당 심판 기관이 정신장애인 본인이 자신의 일을 스스로 책임질 수 없다고 결정했을 때에는, 환자의 상황에 필요하고 적합한 범위 내에서 정신장애인의 이익을 보호하기 위한 조치가 취해져야 한다.

7.1. 만약 개인이 자신의 일을 스스로 책임질 수 없다면 정신장애인의 이익을 보호하기 위해 어떠한 조치가 필요한가?(예를 들면, 후견인, 개인 대리인 또는 피신탁인의 임명)

7.2. 이 대리인의 위탁 의무는 무엇인가? 이러한 위탁 의무를 완수하

지 못했을 때 생기는 결과는 무엇인가? 능력을 상실한 개인을 학대 또는 착취하는 사건이 발생했을 때 행정상·민사상, 그리고/또는 형사상의 처벌이 있는가?

미성년자에 대한 보호
protection of minors

미성년자의 권리 보호를 위해서는 이 UN 원칙의 목적과 미성년자 보호와 관련된 국내법의 범주 안에서 특별한 돌봄이 주어져야 하며, 필요한 경우 가족 구성원 외의 개인 대리인을 선정하는 것도 이에 포함된다.

1. 미성년 정신장애인 보호를 보장하기 위한 특별한 조치가 있다면 무엇인가?

2. 미성년을 판단하는 범주는 무엇인가?

3. 정신보건 전문가는 미성년 정신장애인을 돌보도록 특별한 훈련을 받았는가?

4. 미성년자는 성년이 될 때까지 미성년 기간의 법정 기록을 기밀로 할 수 있는 특별한 권리를 갖는가?

5. 미성년자는 몇 살 때 치료에 동의하는 것을 고지받을 수 있다고 간주되는가? 미성년자는 몇 살 때 정보공개에 관해 동의하는 것을 고지받을 수 있는가? 예를 들어 투표, 군 복무, 배심 의무 등 다른 목적에 대해서 성년으로 판단되는 연령과 차이가 있는가?

6. 가족 구성원 외의 개인 대리인 지정이 가능한가? 가능하다면 어떠한 경우에 가능한가? 가능하지 않다면 학대받거나 착취당하는 가정의 아이들을 위한 특별한 조항이 있는가? 고아가 되거나 유기되거나 또는 법원에서 부모의 양육권 종료를 명령한 경우 등이 발생할 때, 통상적으로 누가 개인 대리인으로 임명되는가?

7. 정신보건 의료 시설 및 지역사회에서 미성년 정신장애인 교육을 위한 규정이 있는가? 있다면 어떤 것인가? 이러한 학교 또는 프로그램들은 지역사회의 다른 일반 학교와 같은 방식으로 인가되는가?

8. 정신적으로 건강하지 않은 미성년자를 위한 특별한 규정이 있는가? 예를 들면 그들의 부모가 병원에 입원해 있거나 부모가 아이를 양육할 능력이 부족하다고 판단될 경우, 그들은 어떻게 보호받는가?

지역사회에서의 삶
life in the community

모든 정신장애인은 가능한 한 지역사회 내에서 생활하고 일할 권리를 가진다.

1. 모든 정신장애인은 의학적으로 안정하다고 가정할 경우 병원 밖에서 거주하고 일할 수 있는가?

2. 정신장애인의 요구에 맞게 생활 여건이 특별히 마련되는가? 그렇다면 지역사회 내에 그들의 요구를 충족할 만큼 충분한 양이 존재하는가? 이러한 시설은 공공시설인가, 또는 민간시설인가?

3. 정신장애인이 병원 밖에서 일하는 것이 가능한가? 그들의 독립을 지원하기 위한 직업 재활 프로그램이 있는가?

4. 이러한 시설 또는 프로그램은 그들이 속해 있는 지역사회의 재정적인 범주 안에서 계획되었는가?

5. 정신보건 의료 시설에서 평균 입원 기간은?
   a. 정해진 시설 내에서는 어떠한가?
   b. 정해진 지역에서는 어떠한가?
   c. 국가 전체로는 어떠한가?

6. 사회적 재통합 활동을 지원하기 위해 하나 또는 그 이상의 기관에 지원될 특별예산이 있는가? 어떻게 할당되는가?

7. 병원에 입원한 동안 또는 퇴원 후의 심리사회적 재활을 위한 조치가 있는가?

8. 지역사회에서 이용 가능한 사회복지 서비스 및 보건 서비스에는 어떤 것이 있는가?

9. 환자들은 퇴원에 앞서 그들이 속한 지역사회의 사회복지 서비스 및 보건 서비스에 익숙해질 기회를 가지는가?

10. 다른 치료 시설, 학교 또는 사회복지 기관과 어떠한 접촉이 이루어지고 있는가?

11. 정신보건 입원 시설에서 퇴원한 후 환자들의 삶과 추후 계획은 무엇인가? 예를 들어 사회 복귀 시설, 생활 지지 아파트(supportive apartment), 지역사회 정신보건 센터, 부분병원(partial hospital) 또는 주간 프로그램, 위기관리 센터 등이 있는가? 그러한 것들은 사회적 재통합을 위한 단계적인 계획의 일부인가?

12. 이러한 시설들은 지역사회의 필요를 충족하기에 충분한가?

13. 이러한 시설들은 보건 당국의 감시를 받는가? 그렇다면 어느 기관인가?

14. 이러한 시설들은 병원과 동일한 방식으로 인가되거나 허가되는가?

15. 만약 이 시설들이 인가서나 허가증을 획득하지 못하게 되면 그 결과는 어떠한가?

16. 정부의 재정적 지원을 받아 개인 소유 주택을 마련할 기회가 있는 가? 예를 들면, 그러한 주택의 건설 및 유지를 위해 발행하는 지방채 가 있는가?

정신장애의 판정
determination of mental illness

1. 개인의 정신장애 판정은 국제적으로 공인된 의학적 기준에 따른다.

  1.1. 정신장애 판정 기준은 무엇인가? (ICD, DSM-IV, 그 외?)
  1.2. 어떤 방법으로 모든 환자가 평가받는가?
    a. 누가 평가를 수행하는가?
    b. 어디에서 평가를 수행하는가?
    c. 다른 평가 방식으로 접근이 가능한가? 예를 들면, 신경계 검사가
       가능한가? 심리 검사가 가능한가? 소변 및 혈액 검사를 위해 갖춰
       진 실험 시설이 있는가? 충분한 설명에 입각해 환자들이 자신의
       검사에 동의했다면, 일반적으로 의료 기록의 열람이 가능한가?

2. 정신장애 판정은 절대로 정치적·경제적·사회적 상황이나 문화, 인종 또는
종교적 소속, 기타 정신 건강 상태와 직접적인 관련이 없는 다른 이유로 결정
되어서는 안 된다.

  2.1. 개인의 정치적·경제적·사회적 상황이 정신장애 진단에 영향을 미
       치는가?
  2.2. 문화, 인종 또는 종교적 소속 여부가 정신장애 진단에 영향을 미
       치는가?
  2.3. 개인의 정신건강 상태와 직접적인 관련이 없는 다른 이유가 정신

장애 진단에 영향을 미치는가?

2.4. 지배적인 도덕적·사회적·문화적·정치적 가치와의 불일치를 정신장애를 진단하는 요소로 고려하는가?

3. 가족이나 직업적 갈등 또는 개인이 속한 사회에서 일반적으로 통용되는 도덕적·사회적·문화적 또는 정치적 가치나 종교적 믿음과의 불일치 등은 절대로 정신장애를 판단하는 기준이 될 수 없다.

3.1. 가족 또는 직업적 갈등이 정신장애를 진단하는 요소로 영향을 미치는가?

3.2. 개인의 정신건강 상태에 직접적인 영향을 주지 않는 다른 요소들을 정신장애의 진단에 고려하는가?

4. 과거에 환자로서 치료받거나 입원한 기록만을 근거로 현재 또는 미래의 정신장애를 판단할 수 없다.

정신장애로 인한 과거의 치료 또는 입원 기록이 현재 또는 미래의 정신장애에 대한 판단을 정당화하는가?

5. 어떠한 개인이나 권한 기관도 정신장애 또는 정신장애의 결과와 직접적으로 관계된 목적을 제외하고는 개인을 정신장애인으로 규정하거나 지목할 수 없다.

요컨대 정신건강 상태와는 다른 이유로 정신장애인으로 진단받은 사람이 있는가? 만약 이러한 경우가 실제로 존재한다면 그 분석 자료를 통해 상관관계를 세울 수 있는가? 예를 들면, 인종·종교·언어·정치적 신념 등과 같은 요소가 포함된 어떤 그룹이 입원되고, 어떤 환경에서 얼마 동안 입원되었는지에 관한 비교 연구가 있는가?

의학 검사
medical examination

국내법에 의해 인정된 절차에 따르는 경우를 제외하고는 그 어떤 개인에게도 자신이 정신장애를 가졌다고 판정할 만한 의학 검사를 받도록 강요할 수 없다.

1. 이에 관한 법적 조치가 결여된 경우, 의학 검사를 받는 것을 강요받은 사람이 있는가?

2. 국내법에 따라 개인이 정신상태검사(Mental Status Examination: MSE)를 강요받을 수 있는가? 만약 그렇다면 언제 그러한가? 예를 들면 응급실 절차의 일부로 포함된 정신상태검사일 수 있다. 그러한 검사는 법적 행위능력, 권한, 친권의 적합성, 가석방 상태 등을 판단하기 위한 법원의 명령에 의해 수행될 것이다.

3. 그러한 검사는 누가 수행하는가?

4. 그러한 검사를 수행하는 데 드는 비용은 누가 지불하는가?

5. 정신상태검사 실시 전에 충분한 설명에 입각하여 동의를 요구하는가? 충분한 설명에 입각한 동의는 정신상태검사에 선행하여 이루어지는가?

6. 환자는 다른 의사의 진단을 요구할 권리, 그리고/또는 기회를 가지는가?

비밀 보장
confidentiality

정보의 비밀이 보장될 권리는 이 UN 원칙이 적용되는 모든 사람들에 대해 존중되어야 한다.

1. 환자 그리고/또는 환자의 기록에 관한 법적 접근성을 가진 모든 사람들은 환자의 비밀 보장 권리를 전적으로 존중하는가?

2. 특별히 누가 비밀 보장을 유지할 의무를 가지는가? 〔자조 그룹(self-help group)이나 정상적인 치료 환경 외부에 누설되는 정보를 고려하라. 치료 시설의 비의료진에게 누설되는 정보를 고려하라.〕

3. 비밀 보장은 어떻게 보호되는가?

4. 환자가 충분히 이해할 수 있는 형식과 언어로 된 문서 형태의 동의 서식이 있고, 정보공개에 앞서 환자 또는 법정 대리인의 서명이 요구되는가?

5. 만약 그렇다면 그러한 동의는 일반적인가, 제한적인가?

6. 만약 제한적이라면 어떤 방식으로 제한받는가? 예를 들면 환자는 그들의 비밀 정보가 전달되는 자를 통제할 수 있는가? 환자는 전달되

는 정보의 내용을 제한할 수 있는가? 환자는 동의에 대한 기간 제한을 둘 수 있는가? 환자는 정보의 사용 목적을 제한할 수 있는가?

7. 환자의 비밀 보장에 대한 권리를 존중하고 보호하지 못할 경우, 그 결과 그리고/또는 처벌은 어떠한가?

8. 비밀 보장이 침해받을 수 있는 경우는 어떤 환경에서인가?

9. 어떤 환경에서 비밀 보장이 지켜지지 않아도 되는가? (비밀 보장이 생명을 위협하는 위급 상황인 경우, 공공의 안전 또는 법원의 명령에 의할 경우 등 비밀 보장의 침해가 정당한 상황인 경우가 포함될 수 있다.)

지역사회와 문화의 역할
role of community and culture

1. 모든 정신장애인은 가능한 한 자신이 거주하는 지역사회에서 치료받고 보살핌을 받을 권리가 있다.

  1.1. 치료받는 지역은 환자의 거주지로부터 얼마나 멀리 있는가?(거리와 일반적인 이동의 어려움 모두 고려하라.) 환자의 거주지와 근접한 곳에 비교 가능한 시설이 있는가?

2. 정신보건 시설에서 치료가 이루어질 때 환자는 가능한 언제나 자신의 거주지 또는 친척이나 친구의 거주지 근처에서 치료받을 권리가 있으며, 가능한 한 치료가 끝나는 즉시 지역사회로 복귀할 권리가 있다.

  2.1. 환자는 치료를 마치고 얼마 후에 지역사회로 복귀하는가?
  2.2. 환자는 어떻게 지역사회로 재통합되는가?(앞의 원칙 3 참조)

3. 모든 정신장애인은 자신이 속한 지역사회의 문화적 배경에 적합한 치료를 받을 권리가 있다.

  3.1. 모든 정신장애인은 자신의 문화적 배경을 고려하여 치료받는가?
  3.2. 이것은 어떻게 보장되는가?
  3.3. 이 원칙의 한계는 무엇인가? 예를 들어 정신분열 진단을 받은

환자가 종교적 배경을 이유로 치료를 거부하고 치료되지 않았을 때, 환자의 종교적 믿음은 존중되는가? 아니면 치료 시설은 치료를 위한 법적 동의를 얻기 위해 후견인 지정을 요청할 수 있는가?

돌봄의 기준
standard of care

1. 모든 정신장애인은 자신의 보건의료 필요에 적합한 보건 및 사회적 의료를 받을 권리가 있으며, 기타 질환자와 동일한 기준의 돌봄과 치료를 받을 권리가 있다.

    1.1. 질 보장 기준이 장려되는가? 그렇다면 어떤 기준인가?[2]

    1.2. 신체장애나 신체적 질환을 가진 사람과 비교할 때, 정신장애나 정신 질환을 가진 사람을 위한 사회적 돌봄 및 건강 돌봄의 기준에 차이가 있는가?

    1.3. 모든 정신장애인은 자신의 보건의료 필요에 적합한 보건의료 및 복지 서비스를 받는가?

    1.4. 신체 질환을 가진 사람과 비교할 때 돌봄의 기준은 무엇인가?

    1.5. 만약 환자가 자신의 건강을 돌볼 수 없다면 그들은 이에 대해 도움을 받는가?

    1.6. 외래 환자의 경우, 정신보건 전문가를 만나려면 어느 정도의 시간이 걸리는가?

    1.7. 응급 처치를 위해 어떠한 절차가 적절한가?

    1.8. 정신장애인은 입원 중 정기적으로 충분한 의학 검사를 받는가? 그렇지 않다면 언제 검사를 받는가? 아니면 전혀 받지 않는가?

---

2) WHO – Division of Mental Health, "Quality Assurance in Mental Health Care (Vol. 1)"(1994) 참조.

1.9. 그 후 만성 또는 급성 환자의 의학 검사의 빈도는 어떠한가?

1.10. 모든 환자들은 자신의 고유 공간을 가지고 있는가?

1.11. 정신장애의 치료를 위한 필수 의약품을 이용할 수 있는가? (다음의 원칙 10 참조)

2. 모든 환자들은 적절하지 못한 약물 치료, 다른 환자나 직원 또는 다른 사람들로부터의 학대, 또는 정신적 불안이나 신체적 불편을 야기하는 기타 행동 등의 위해로부터 보호받아야 한다.

2.1. 환자들은 적절하지 못한 약물 치료 등의 위해로부터 어떻게 보호받는가?

2.2. 치료의 양상은 어떻게 모니터링되는가? 치료 결정, 특히 강박과 격리를 위한 약물 치료 심사 및 계획은 여러 전문 분야에 걸친 직원회의를 통해 논의되는가?

2.3. 치료 결정은 정기적으로 심사되는가? 그렇다면 그 간격은? 그렇지 않다면 어떻게 이루어지는가? 모든 직원들은 심폐소생술과 기본적인 응급 처치뿐만 아니라 적절하고 강박이 최소한으로 제한되는 방식을 교육받는가? (다음의 2.11.~2.14. 참조)

2.4. 어떤 형태의 강박이 허용되며, 어떤 형태가 허용되지 않는가?

2.5. 격리나 강박의 행사에 대한 문서화된 절차가 있는가?

2.6. 간호 직원이 '필요한 만큼' 약물을 복용시키는 것과 같은 투약 규칙이 있는가? 그렇다면 이는 직원의 편의를 위해 남용되는가?

2.7. 모든 직원들은 정기적으로 다른 직원들로부터 관리·감독을 받는가?

2.8. 환자는 다른 환자나 직원들에 의한 학대로부터 어떻게 보호

받는가?

2.9. 폭력적인 환자는 비폭력적인 환자들과 함께 입원되는가?

2.10. 주간 근무 중 직원 대비 환자의 비율은 어떠한가? 야간 근무 중 직원 대비 환자의 비율은 어떠한가? 이러한 비율은 병동이나 병실의 필요를 충족하기에 적당한가?

2.11. 병실은 환자 과잉 상태인가?

2.12. '날카로운 물건'과 같은 위험한 물건 또는 제재에 대한 규정은 무엇인가? 폐쇄 구역 또는 접근 금지 구역에 보관하는가?

2.13. 환자들의 개인 물품을 입원 시 및 입원 후에 수색하는가?

2.14. 모든 환자들은 입원에 앞서 전염성 질환에 관한 검사를 받는가? 인체면역결핍바이러스(HIV)의 경우, 환자의 인권 침해 가능성이 고려되는가? 보편적인 예방 조치가 준수되는가? 환자들 간 또는 환자와 직원들 간의 가까운 접촉에 대해 안전 조치가 취해지는가?

치료
treatment

1. 모든 정신장애인은 환자의 건강 관련 필요와 다른 이들의 신체적 안전을 보호하기 위해 필요한 치료로서 가능한 한 제한적이지 않은 치료를 받을 권리를 가진다.

> 1.1. 환자는 가능한 제한적이지 않은 환경에서 의학적으로 필요한 치료를 받고, 제한적이거나 강제적이지 않은 형태로 의학적으로 필요한 치료를 받는가? (원칙 8의 2.2.~2.3. 참조)
>
> 1.2. 구속에 대한 필요성을 얼마나 자주 재평가하는가?

2. 모든 환자들에 대한 치료 및 의료는 환자에 따라 개별적으로 처방된 계획에 기초해야 하며, 환자와 함께 논의하고 정기적으로 심사하며 필요할 때마다 수정을 거쳐 자격을 갖춘 전문가에 의해 제공되어야 한다.

> 2.1. 치료 및 의료에 관해 환자마다 개별적으로 처방된 계획이 있는가?
>
> 2.2. 환자와의 의견 조율이 있는가? 환자는 치료 계획에 서명하는가?
>
> 2.3. 환자 또는 개인의 대리인이 동의한 후, 환자의 돌봄에 관해 가족과 의논하는가?
>
> 2.4. 환자는 자신의 건강 상태의 경과에 관해 충분히 전해 듣는가?
>
> 2.5. 치료 계획은 몇 차례나 심사하는가? 치료 계획을 주기적으로 자동 심사하는가?

2.6. 환자의 돌봄 계획을 상의하기 위해 직원회의는 몇 차례나 열리는가?

2.7. 필요에 따라 치료 계획이 수정되는가?

2.8. 누가 치료를 제공하는가?

2.9. 치료 계획은 환자의 문화, 종교, 임상 상태, 연령에 적합한가?

3. 정신보건 의료는 UN 총회가 채택한 「수감자 및 억류자들을 고문과 기타 잔인하거나 비인간적인 대우 및 처벌로부터 보호하기 위한 보건 종사자, 특히 의사들의 역할에 관한 의학 윤리 원칙」과 같이 국제적으로 인증된 기준을 비롯해 정신보건 종사자들을 위한 윤리로 적용할 수 있는 기준들에 따라 제공되어야 한다.

3.1. 정신보건 제공자들이 참조하는 윤리 기준은 무엇인가?

3.2. 정신보건 의료 제공자들이 고문 또는 기타 잔인하고 비인간적이거나 수준 낮은 처우나 처벌을 시행했음을 제시할 증거가 있는가?

3.3. 정신보건 의료 제공자들이 환자가 고문 또는 기타 잔인하고 비인간적이며 낮은 수준의 처우를 받았다는 것을 인지했을 때, 지방정부법에 의거해 보고하도록 되어 있는가? 누구에게 보고해야 하는가?

3.4. 정신장애인이 일반 환자들에 비해 더 자주 학대받았다는 증거가 있는가? 그러한 학대로부터 보호할 수 있는 보호 수단은 무엇인가? (앞의 원칙 8의 2항 참고)

3.5. 실시 중인 윤리 기준 위반에 대한 결과는 무엇인가?

4. 모든 환자의 치료는 반드시 개인적 자율성을 지켜주고 강화하는 방향으로 진행되어야 한다.

4.1. 모든 환자의 치료는 환자의 자율성을 지켜주고 강화하는가?

4.2. 이 목적을 위해 환자의 권리는 보호되는가?

4.3. 개인의 역량 강화는 치료의 우선 사항인가? (앞의 원칙 8의 1.9. 참고)

4.4. 외래 환자의 치료가 입원 환자의 치료에 우선하는가?

4.5. 지역사회 기반 치료가 시설 치료에 우선하는가?

4.6. 지역사회에 지지적인 생활환경이 존재하며 병원 밖에서 생활할 수 있는 환자들에게 그러한 기회가 제공되는가?

약물 치료
medication

1. 약물 치료는 환자의 건강 관련 필요에 최대한 부합해야 하고, 진단상 또는 치료상의 목적을 위해서만 이루어져야 하며, 처벌이나 다른 이들의 편의를 위해 시행되어서는 안 된다. 다음의 원칙 11의 15항에 따라 정신보건 전문가는 그 효능이 이미 밝혀져 있거나 증명된 약물 치료만을 시행해야 한다.

1.1. 증상 및 약물 요법의 사용에 대한 문서화된 지침이 있는가?

1.2. 약물 요법의 사용은 국제적으로 인증된 정신보건 의료에 관한 지침3)을 따르는가?

1.3. 모든 치료 약물은 효능이 이미 밝혀져 있거나 증명되었는가? 그것은 국내법에 의해 사용이 승인되었는가? 모든 약물은 그것이 사용되는 특정한 목적에 관해 승인받는가?

1.4. 약물 치료가 처벌이나 다른 이의 편의를 위해 시행된 적이 있는가?

1.5. 약물 치료가 치료와 진단의 목적을 위해서만 사용된다는 것이 어떻게 보장되는가?

2. 모든 약물 치료는 반드시 법적으로 허가받은 정신보건 전문가에 의해 시행되어야 하며 환자 기록에 기록되어야 한다.

---

3) 예를 들면, WHO, "Essential Drugs in Psychiatry"(1994).

2.1. 약물의 처방 및 조제는 누구의 책임인가?

2.2. 직원들이 환자의 약물 치료에 관한 결정에 참여하는가?

2.3. 모든 약물 치료 내용은 기록되는가? 누가 기록하는가?

2.4. 약물 치료에 관한 사항은 어디에 기록되는가?

2.5. 어떤 의약품이 정신보건 시설의 기본 공급 약품에 포함되는가?

2.6. 어떤 정신과 약품이 기본 공급 약품에 포함되는가?

2.7. 공급되는 약품은 세계보건기구에 등록된 정신에 영향을 미치는 (psychoactive) 필수 의약품4)을 포함하는가?

2.8. 도보로 한 시간 거리 내에서 어떤 신경정신과 약품을 구할 수 있는가?

2.9. 누가 그것을 처방하는가?

2.10. 조제의 성분은 무엇인가? 의원, 병원, 환자의 집, 그룹 홈(group home) 및 생활 지지 아파트에서 약물이 투약되는가?

2.11. 올바른 투약을 보장하기 위해 어떠한 질 보증 조치가 이루어지는가?

2.12. 어떠한 추후 관리 서비스가 제공되는가? 예를 들면, 리튬 수치를 측정하기 위해 정기적인 혈액 샘플 채취가 이루어지는가? 자살 방지를 위해 정기적으로 우울증 환자를 관찰하는가? 추체외로증후군(EPS) 때문에 항정신 약물을 투여받는 환자들을 정기적으로 주시하는가?

2.13. 약물의 도난이나 인증되지 않은 사용을 막기 위해 일상 약물의 재고 파악이 이루어지는가? 이는 별도의 사람들에 의해 수행되는가?

---

4) 아미트리프탈린, 이미프라민, 비페리덴, 카바마제핀, 클로르프로마진, 할로페리돌, 클로미프라민, 디아제팜, 플루페나진, 리튬카보네이트, 페노바르비탈. WHO, "The Use of Essential Drug"(1995), WHO Technical Report Series No. 850.

치료에 대한 동의
consent to treatment

1. 정신장애인의 고지된 동의 없이는 환자를 치료할 수 없다. 단, 이 원칙의 6·7·8·13·15항에 제시된 사항은 예외로 한다.

> 1.1. 치료 전에 고지된 동의가 요구되는가?
>
> 1.2. 치료에 앞서 환자는 고지된 동의를 하는가? 그렇지 않다면 환자의 동의 거부는 존중되는가, 아니면 환자의 의도에 반하여 치료가 이루어지는가?
>
> 1.3. 환자는 치료 동의서에 서명하도록 요구받는가? 일반적으로 환자는 동의서에 서명하는가?
>
> 1.4. 환자 자신의 동의 없이는 불법적으로 치료가 진행될 수 없다는 점을 환자에게 고지하는가?
>
> 1.5. 환자는 동의를 번복할 수 있다는 사실을 고지받는가?
>
> 1.6. 동의는 어떻게 얻어지는가?

2. 고지된 동의란, 다음 사항에 대해 이해 가능하며 적합한 정보를 환자가 이해할 수 있는 언어와 형식으로 환자에게 공개한 뒤 위협이나 부적절한 유도 없이 자유롭게 얻는 동의를 말한다.

(a) 진단 평가

(b) 제안된 치료의 목적과 방법, 예상되는 기간 및 이익

(c) 덜 침해적인 치료법 등 대안적인 치료 방식

(d) 제안된 치료법에 의해 생길 수 있는 고통이나 불편, 위험 및 부작용

2.1. 환자는 자유롭게 치료에 동의할 수 있는 권리를 가지는가? 치료에 관한 동의를 이끌어내기 위한 위협 또는 부적절한 유도가 있는가? (예를 들면, 치료에 관해 환자의 접근을 제한하는 과도한 위험, 환자의 생활 여건을 바꾸는 부당한 위험, 보험자 진료비 부담을 줄이기 위해 한물간 치료 방법을 지나치게 권유하는 것 등을 포함)

2.2. 환자는 진단 평가에 관해 고지받는가?

2.3. 환자는 제안된 치료의 목적, 방법, 예상되는 기간 및 이익에 관해 고지받는가?

2.4. 환자는 대안적인 치료 방법을 고지받는가?

2.5. 환자는 제안된 치료법에 의해 생길 수 있는 고통이나 불편, 위험 및 부작용을 고지받는가?

2.6. 이러한 정보는 어떠한 형식이나 언어로 전달되는가?

2.7. 모든 정보는 적절한 언어로 서면으로 존재하는가? 그렇다면 그 문서는 환자에게 전달되는가? 환자 본인이 읽을 수 있는가? 그렇지 않다면 그 문서를 환자에게 읽어주는가?

2.8. 환자에게 더 적절한 정보를 전달하기 위해 어떠한 장치들이 사용되는가?

2.9. 환자는 고지된 동의를 하기에 적합한 역량을 갖추었는가? 그렇지 않다면 누가 동의하는가? 지방정부법에 의거한 추천된 개인 또는 기관인가? (앞의 원칙 1의 6항 참조)

3. 환자는 동의 절차에 자신이 선택한 1인 또는 다수의 제3자의 동석을 요구할 수 있다.

3.1. 환자는 동의 절차에 자신이 선택한 1인 또는 다수의 제3자의 동석을 요구할 수 있는 권리와 시간을 부여받는가?

3.2. 동의 절차에 누가 참석하는가?

3.3. 환자는 동의 절차에 앞서 비공식적으로 1인 또는 여러 사람의 조언을 구할 수 있는가?

4. 이 원칙의 6·7·8·13·15항에 규정된 사항을 제외하고 환자는 치료를 중단하거나 거부할 권리를 가진다. 치료를 중단 또는 거부할 경우에 발생하는 결과에 대해 환자에게 반드시 설명해야 한다.

4.1. 환자는 치료를 거부하거나 중지할 권리가 있음을 고지받는가?

4.2. 환자는 치료를 거부 또는 중지할 경우 발생하는 결과에 대해 고지받는가?

4.3. 환자는 치료 거부에 대한 보복을 두려워하는가?

4.4. 치료는 강제적으로 이루어질 수 있는가? 그렇다면 언제 그러한가?

4.5. 모든 비자발적 치료(그리고 그것의 정당성)는 환자 기록에 기록되는가?

5. 환자에게 고지된 동의권을 포기하도록 권하거나 유도해서는 안 된다. 환자가 동의권을 포기하려 할 경우에는 고지된 동의 없이는 치료를 할 수 없다는 사실을 환자에게 설명해야 한다.

5.1. 환자는 고지된 동의권을 포기하도록 권유당하거나 유도당하는가?

5.2. 이러한 관례를 막을 보호 장치는 무엇인가?

6. 이 원칙의 7·8·12·13·14·15항의 경우를 제외하고는 다음 조건이 만족될 경우 제안된 치료 계획을 환자에게 고지된 동의 없이 실행할 수 있다.

(a) 해당 시기에 환자가 비자발적 환자로 수용되어 있는 경우

(b) 이 원칙의 2항에 지정된 정보를 포함하여 모든 관련 정보를 갖고 있는 독립적 권한 기관에서, 해당 시기에 환자가 제안된 치료안에 대한 고지된 동의를 하거나 보류할 능력이 없다고 판단하거나, 환자 개인의 안전 또는 타인의 안전과 관련해 해당 환자의 동의 보류가 합당하지 않다고 판단한 경우

(c) 독립적 권한 기관에서 제안된 치료안이 환자의 건강 관련 필요의 해결을 위해 최선이라고 판단한 경우

6.1. 치료가 동의 없이 이루어지는가? 그렇다면 언제 그러한가?

6.2. 만약 치료가 고지된 동의 없이 이루어졌다면, 다음 세 조건을 만족하는가?

　a. 환자가 비자발적 환자인가?

　b. 독립적 권한 기관이 해당 환자가 동의 또는 보류할 능력이 없다고 판단하거나 해당 환자의 보류가 합당하지 않다고 판단하는가?

　c. 독립적 권한 기관에서 제안된 치료안이 환자의 건강 관련 필요의 해결을 위해 최선이라고 판단하는가?

6.3. 모든 치료 사례 중 강제로 치료가 이루어진 경우의 비율은 얼마나 되는가?

6.4. 자발적 치료와 비자발적 치료의 장기적인 치료 효과를 보여주는 연구나 자료가 있는가?

6.5. 법적 행위능력의 회복 가능성은 무엇인가? 그것이 가능한가? 그렇다면 치료의 연기로 인해 과도한 손해가 발생하지 않을 경우에 한해

법적 행위능력이 회복될 때까지 계획된 치료를 연기할 수 있는가? (다음의 9항 참조)

7. 앞의 6항은 환자를 위한 치료에 동의할 개인 대리인이 법에 의해 선임된 환자에게는 적용되지 않는다. 단, 12·13·14·15항에서와 같이 이 원칙의 2항에 기술된 정보를 제공받은 개인 대리인이 환자를 대신해 동의한 경우에는 환자 자신의 고지된 동의 없이 환자를 치료할 수 있다.

  7.1. 개인 대리인은 환자를 대신해 다음 사항에 대해 동의할 권한을 가지는가?
    a. 불임 시술
    b. 진료 또는 수술 절차
    c. 정신장애를 위한 정신외과적 치료 또는 기타 강제적이고 되돌릴 수 없는 치료
    d. 임상 시험 및 실험적 치료
  7.2. 개인 대리인이 동의를 보류한다면, 이러한 결정은 존중되는가?
  7.3. 개인 대리인 그리고/또는 그의 결정과 관련해 이의를 제기할 수 있는 절차가 있는가? 누가 이의를 제기하는가? 환자, 치료 시설, 임상의, 환자의 가족 구성원 등이 포함될 수 있다.

8. 이 원칙의 12·13·14·15항의 내용을 제외하고, 법에 의해 자격을 갖춘 정신보건 전문가가 환자 및 다른 사람들의 직접적이고 절박한 위해를 막기 위해 위급하게 필요하다고 판단할 경우 환자의 고지된 동의 없이 치료를 행할 수 있다. 이러한 치료는 해당 목적에 반드시 필요한 기간을 초과해 연장되어서는 안 된다.

8.1. 누가 위급 상황의 상태를 판단하는가? 한 개인을 비자발적으로 치료하기 위해 얼마나 많은 서명이 필요한가? 누구의 서명이 필요한가?

8.2. 위급 상황으로 판단할 때 어떤 사항이 고려되는가? 위급 또는 긴급 상황의 개념은 자신 또는 타인에게 절박한 위험일 경우로 제한되는가? 그렇지 않다면 어떤 기준이 적용되는가?

8.3. 긴급 비자발적 치료의 범주는 특히 다음 사항을 제외하는가?

　a. 불임 시술

　b. 정신장애를 위한 정신외과적 치료 또는 기타 강제적이고 되돌릴 수 없는 치료

　c. 임상 시험 및 실험적 치료

8.4. 이와 같은 치료는 어느 정도 연장되는가?

8.5. 비자발적 치료의 실행에 법원의 명령이 필요한가?

8.6. 비자발적 치료의 실행에 대한 시간적 제한은 얼마 동안인가? 법률에 의해 정해지고 주기적으로 재고되는가? 아니면 시간제한은 법원, 개인 대리인 또는 비자발적 치료의 실행을 감독하는 의사에 의해 결정되는가?

9. 환자의 고지된 동의 없이 치료가 승인되는 경우라 하더라도, 치료의 성격과 가능한 대안에 관해 환자에게 알리고 치료안의 전개에 가능한 한 환자를 참여시키도록 최대한 노력해야 한다.

9.1. 환자의 동의 없이 치료가 이루어졌다 하더라도 환자는 부작용을 포함한 치료의 성격과 가능한 대안에 대해 고지받는가?

9.2. 가능한 범위에서 환자는 치료 계획의 개발에 어떻게 관여하는가?

10. 모든 치료는 자발성 또는 비자발성 표시와 함께 환자의 의료 기록에 즉시 기록되어야 한다.

 10.1. 모든 치료가 기록되는가?

 10.2. 어떤 형식으로 기록되는가?

 10.3. 어디에 기록되는가?

 10.4. 언제 기록되는가?

 10.5. 누구에 의해 기록되는가?

 10.6. 특히 약물 치료와 관련한 문서화에 관해 승인된 기준이 있는가?

11. 환자의 신체적 강박이나 비자발적 격리는 환자나 다른 사람들의 직접적이고 절박한 위해를 막기 위한 유일한 수단인 경우에 한해, 반드시 해당 정신보건 시설에서 공식적으로 승인된 절차에 따라서 사용되어야 한다. 또한 이같은 목적에 반드시 필요한 기간을 초과해 연장되어서는 안 된다. 모든 신체적 강박이나 비자발적 격리 사례는 그 이유와 성격, 범위를 환자의 의료 기록에 기록해야만 한다. 강박 및 격리된 환자는 인도적인 환경에 처해야 하며, 자격을 갖춘 의료진이 정기적으로 세밀하게 감독하고 보살펴야 한다. 관련된 개인 대리인이 있는 경우 환자의 신체적 강박이나 비자발적 격리에 대해 반드시 즉시 통보해야 한다.

 11.1. 어떠한 환경에서 신체적 강박이나 비자발적 격리가 사용되는가?

 11.2. 신체적 강박이나 비자발적 격리를 취하는 명확한 목적은 무엇인가?

 11.3. 환자는 얼마 동안 강박되거나 격리되는가? 이러한 행위는 필요한 기간 동안만으로 제한되는가?

11.4. 모든 신체적 강박이나 비자발적 격리 사례는 문서화되는가? 이러한 기록에는 강박 또는 격리의 정당성과 성격, 범위가 포함되는가? 이러한 문서는 어디에 보관되는가?

11.5. 어떤 환경에서 환자가 강박되는가?

11.6. 환자의 신체적 강박이나 비자발적 격리는 누구에게 통보되는가? 얼마 후에 통보되는가?

12. 불임 시술은 정신장애 치료로 절대 행할 수 없다.

12.1. 정신장애 치료의 일환으로 불임 시술이 행해지는가? 그렇다면 어떤 상황에서 행해지는가?

12.2. 이러한 사건이 최근에 몇 차례나 발생했는가? (예를 들어 지난 18개월 동안)

12.3. 과거에 비해 이런 일이 더 빈번히 발생하는 편인가?

12.4. 기타 일정한 목적을 가지고 어떤 단체에서 불임 시술이 비정상적으로 치료의 일환으로 행해지는가?

13. 위험성이 있는 약물 치료나 수술은 국내법에 의해 허가되는 경우에 한해서, 환자의 건강을 위한 최선의 방법이라고 여겨지며 환자가 고지된 동의를 했을 때만 시술할 수 있다. 환자가 고지된 동의를 할 능력이 없는 경우에는 독립적인 심사가 이루어진 후에만 시술을 허가할 수 있다.

13.1. 정신장애인에게 주요 의학적 또는 수술적 절차가 시행되는 경우, 환자는 고지된 동의를 하는가?

13.2. 환자가 고지된 동의를 할 능력이 없는 경우에는 어떠한가?

13.3. 이러한 절차를 밟는 이유는 무엇인가?

13.4. 이러한 과정은 즉시 필요한가, 아니면 독립적으로 이러한 결정을 할 수 있는 법적 행위능력을 회복할 때까지 환자에게 과도한 손해를 입히지 않는 선에서 연기될 수 있는가? 누가 이것을 판단하는가?

14. 정신장애에 대한 정신과 수술 및 기타 번복할 수 없는 침해적인 치료는 정신보건 시설에 비자발적으로 수용되어 있는 환자에게는 행할 수 없다. 또한 다른 환자들에 대해서도, 국내법에 의해 허용되는 범위에서 이미 환자가 고지된 동의를 한 상태에서 외부의 독립적인 기관이 고지된 동의가 있었음을 인정하고 환자의 건강 관련 필요에 해당 치료가 최선이라고 판단한 경우에만 행할 수 있다.

14.1. 언제 정신과 수술 및 기타 번복할 수 없는 침해적인 치료가 통상적으로 행해지는가?

14.2. 그 환자가 비자발적인 환자가 아니라는 것이 보장되는가?

14.3. 누가 이를 승인하는가?

14.4. 후견인이나 개인 대리인의 권한이 여기까지 확장될 수 있는가?

15. 임상 시험 및 실험적 치료는 고지된 동의 없이 시술될 수 없다. 단, 이 같은 목적을 위해 설립된 독립적인 해당 심사 기관의 승인이 있는 경우, 고지된 동의를 할 수 없는 환자를 임상 시험 또는 실험적 치료에 포함시킬 수 있다.

15.1. 정신장애인이 임상 시험 또는 실험적 치료에 참여하는가? 그렇다면 언제 참여하는가?

15.2. 고지된 동의가 필요한가?(1항 참조) 환자가 고지된 동의를 하는가?

15.3. 환자가 동의를 할 수 없는 상황이라면, 누가 승인하는가?

15.4. 개인 대리인이나 후견인은 임상 시험 또는 실험적 치료에 환자가 참여하는 것에 관해 동의할 수 있는 권한을 가지는가?

16. 이 원칙의 6·7·8·13·14·15항에 해당하는 경우, 환자나 그의 개인 대리인 또는 이해관계인에게는 환자가 받는 치료에 대해 사법기관 및 기타 독립적인 권한 기관에 이의를 제기할 수 있는 권리가 주어져야 한다.

16.1. 환자는 고지된 동의 없이 치료를 받는가?(1항 참조)

16.2. 정신과 수술 및 기타 번복할 수 없는 침해적인 치료가 환자에게 시행되는가?

16.3. 만약 위의 16.1.과 16.2.에 대한 답이 '예'일 경우, 누가 권한 기관에 이의를 제기할 권리를 가지는가? 취해진 행위가 정당화되지 않거나 부적절하게 승인되었다고 법원이 판단할 경우, 그러한 판결의 결과는 무엇인가? 예를 들어 환자에게 번복할 수 없는 치료가 행해진 경우, 환자나 그의 가족은 치료 시설 그리고/또는 의사를 상대로 민사 소송을 제기할 수 있는가? 이러한 치료 행위는 불법으로 간주되는가? 그렇다면 그 치료 과정이 단지 번복할 수 없이 침해적이라는 이유로 치료 시설이나 의사, 또는 둘 모두를 대상으로 형사처분을 강행할 수 있는가?

16.4. 이러한 이의를 제기하기에 적절한 권한 기관은 어디인가?

권리에 대한 고지
notice of rights

1. 정신보건 시설에 입원하는 환자에게는 입원 즉시 가능한 한 빨리, 이 UN 원칙과 국내법에 따른 자신의 모든 권리를 환자가 이해할 수 있는 언어와 형식으로 고지해야 하며, 그 정보에는 이들 권리에 대한 설명과 권리 행사 방법이 포함되어야 한다.

   1.1. 정신보건 시설에 입원한 환자는 자신의 모든 권리를 고지받는가?

   1.2. 언제 환자가 고지받는가?

   1.3. 환자는 이러한 정보를 환자가 이해할 수 있는 언어와 형식으로 고지받는가?

   1.4. 환자는 이러한 권리를 행사할 방법을 알고 있는가?

   1.5. 필수적인 법적 행위능력을 갖춘 환자는 자신을 대신해 권리를 고지받을 개인을 지정할 권리를 가지는가?

   1.6. 환자는 시설의 권한에 대해 자신의 권익을 대표할 사람을 지정할 권리를 가지는가?

   1.7. 환자는 자신의 권리 행사와 관련해 처벌이나 합법적 보복의 두려움으로부터 자유로운가?

   1.8. 환자가 그러한 정보를 이해할 수 없는 경우, 누가 환자를 대신해 고지받는가?

2. 이러한 정보를 환자가 이해할 수 없을 때에는 개인 대리인이 있는 경우

개인 대리인과 환자의 권익을 가장 잘 대변할 수 있고 또 그렇게 하려는 사람(들)에게 환자의 권리를 알려야 한다.

2.1. 누가 환자를 대신해 고지받는가?
2.2. 누가 권한을 가지고 환자를 대표하는가?
  a. 친구
  b. 지정된 개인 대리인

3. 해당 행위능력이 있는 환자는 시설에 대해 자신의 이익을 대변할 사람과 자신을 대신해 정보를 고지받을 사람을 지정할 권리를 가진다.

3.1. 누가 이런 대리인을 임명하는가?
3.2. 이러한 개인 대리인의 권한에 대한 실질적이고 일시적인 제한은 무엇인가? (앞의 원칙 1의 7항 참조)

정신보건 시설에서의 권리와 조건
rights and conditions in mental health facilities

1. 정신보건 시설에 입원한 모든 환자들은 특히 다음 사항에 대해 전적으로 존중받을 권리를 가진다.

　(a) 언제나 법 앞에서 평등한 인간으로서의 인정

　(b) 사생활

　(c) 의사소통 및 통신의 자유: 여기에는 시설 내 다른 사람들과 소통할 자유, 검열 없이 사적인 서신을 주고받을 자유, 사적으로 대리인이나 개인 대리인의 방문을 받을 자유, 합당한 시간이라면 언제나 기타 면회인을 만날 자유, 우편 및 전화와 신문·라디오·TV를 이용할 자유 등이 포함된다.

　(d) 종교 또는 사상의 자유

1.1. 정신보건 의료에 대해 국제적으로 공인된 지침을 따르고 있는가?[5]

1.2. 환자가 법 앞에서 평등한 인간으로서 충분히 존중받는가?

1.3. 환자의 사생활이 충분히 존중받는가? 예를 들면,

　a. 화장실과 욕실의 문은 안에서 잠글 수 있는가?

　b. 만약 신체검사나 소변검사가 필요할 경우, 환자의 사생활이 충분히 존중받는가?

1.4. 환자의 성에 관한 자기 결정은 충분히 존중되는가? 환자에 대한 성적 추행 및 학대가 묵인되는가?

---

5) WHO, "Essential Treatments in Psychiatry"(1994) 참조.

1.5. 환자의 의사소통의 자유는 충분히 존중되는가? 예를 들면,

  a. 환자는 시설의 다른 사람들과 의사소통할 권리를 가지는가?

  b. 환자는 검열 없이 사적인 서신을 자유롭게 보내거나 받을 수 있는가?

  c. 환자는 사적으로 대리인이나 개인 대리인 및 기타 방문자들의 방문을 받을 자유가 있는가?

1.6. 환자는 자신의 종교 또는 사상을 표현하고 실천하는 데 자유로운가?

1.7. 환자는 신문, 라디오와 TV를 이용하는 데 자유로운가?

2. 정신보건 시설 내의 환경 및 생활 조건은 비슷한 연령의 일반인의 생활과 최대한 유사해야 하며, 특히 다음을 포함해야 한다.

(a) 오락 및 여가 활동을 위한 시설

(b) 교육 시설

(c) 일상생활과 오락, 통신에 필요한 물건을 구입하거나 받을 수 있는 시설

(d) 환자가 자신의 사회적·문화적 배경에 맞는 직업을 갖도록 도움을 주는 시설과 지역사회로의 복귀를 촉진할 수 있는 적절한 직업 재활을 위한 시설, 그리고 그러한 시설 사용에 대한 장려. 이러한 방법들은 환자가 지역사회에서 직업을 얻거나 유지하도록 도와주는 직업 안내, 직업 훈련 및 배치 서비스를 포함해야 한다.

2.1. 정신 치료 시설 내의 생활 조건은 비슷한 연령의 일반인의 생활과 유사한가?

2.2. 정신보건 시설에서 오락 및 여가 활동을 위해 가능한 것은 무엇인가?

2.3. 교육을 위해 가능한 것은 무엇인가? 미성년자 교육을 위한 특별한 필요조건이 있는가? (원칙 2의 7. 참조)

2.4. 환자들은 일상생활, 오락 및 통신에 필요한 물건을 구입하거나 받을 수 있는가?

2.5. 환자들의 실질적인 직업을 위해 마련된 가능한 것은 무엇인가? 그 직업은 환자의 사회적·문화적 배경에 적합한가?

2.6. 환자의 이용 가능한 활동 범위를 규정하는 지침이 존재하는가?

2.7. 환자들이 이러한 가능한 것들을 이용하도록 어떻게 장려하는가?

3. 어떠한 경우에도 환자에게 강압적인 노동을 시켜서는 안 된다. 시설 운영의 요건에 부합하고 환자의 욕구에 부응하는 한계 내에서, 환자가 자신이 원하는 작업의 유형을 선택할 수 있어야 한다.

3.1. 환자가 일하기를 원하는 경우, 환자는 수행하려는 작업의 유형을 선택할 수 있는가?

3.2. 환자가 강압적인 무임금 노동을 강요받는가?

3.3. 환자는 자신의 노동에 대해 어떤 보상을 받는가? 어떤 형태로 보상받는가? (앞의 원칙 1의 4항, 4.4. 참조)

4. 정신보건 시설 환자의 노동이 착취당해서는 안 된다. 시설 환자들은 자신이 하는 일에 대해 정상인이 국내법이나 관습에 따라 같은 일에 대해 받는 것과 같은 수준의 보수를 받을 권리를 가진다. 또한 환자가 한 일에 대해 정신보건 시설에 보수가 지불된 경우에는 반드시 이 중 합당한 몫을 받을 권리가 있다.

4.1. 지역사회로의 재통합을 촉진하기 위해 무엇이 행해지는가?

4.2. 심리사회적 재활을 위해 어떠한 조치가 취해지는가?

4.3. 직업 안내 및 직업 훈련이 있는가?

4.4. 환자들이 지역사회에서 직업을 얻고 이를 유지할 수 있는 배치 서비스가 있는가?

4.5. 다음 사항들과 정신보건 시설은 어떤 관계가 있는가?

- 환자들의 고용주
- 정신보건 시설 지역에 있는 학교와 기타 사회복지 기관

정신보건 시설의 자원
resources for mental health facilities

1. 정신보건 시설은 특히 다음 사항을 포함하여 다른 보건 시설과 같은 수준의
자원을 갖추어야 한다.

  (a) 의학 및 기타 적합한 전문적 자격을 갖춘 직원의 수가 충분해야 하며,
모든 환자들이 사생활을 보호받을 수 있을 만큼 충분한 공간과 적절하고
능동적인 치료 프로그램

  (b) 환자의 진단 및 치료 시설

  (c) 적절한 전문적 의료

  (d) 약물 치료 제공 등 적합하고 정기적이며 종합적인 치료

1.1. 다른 보건 시설과 비교하여 정신보건 시설의 자원은 어떠한가?
신체장애를 위한 치료와 비교하여 정신보건 치료에 대한 접근은 어떠
한가?

1.2. 직원/환자 비율은?(일반적으로, 그리고 특히 일정한 시설 내에서)

1.3. 바람직한 치료 과정, 여가 활동 및 방문객 접견 등을 위해 적합한
공간이 있는가?(일반적으로, 그리고 특히 일정한 시설 내에서)

1.4. 각 환자는 사생활이 보장된 적절하고 활동적인 치료를 제공받는
가?(일반적으로, 그리고 특히 일정한 시설 내에서)

1.5. 정신보건 서비스의 재정은 어떤 식으로든 정치적인 충성이나 신
조에 예속되는가?

1.6. 정신보건 서비스는 종교적 믿음 또는 계파에 종속적인가?

2. 해당 기관에서는 모든 정신보건 시설을 적당한 빈도로 검열하여, 환자들에 대한 조건과 치료 및 의료가 이 UN 원칙에 부합하도록 해야 한다.

2.1. 누구에 의해 정신보건 시설이 검열을 받는가?
2.2. 얼마나 자주 검열을 받는가?
2.3. 인가를 위한 필요조건과 그 절차는 무엇인가? 사용된 기준은 무엇인가? 인가 및 미인가의 결과는 어떠한가?
2.4. 인가가 거부되는 기관의 비율은 어느 정도인가?

입원 원칙
admission principles

1. 정신보건 시설 내 치료가 필요한 사람이 있을 경우, 비자발적 입원을 피하기 위해 모든 노력을 기울여야 한다.

> 1.1. 자발적 입원 절차가 이용 가능하며 행해지고 있는가?
>
> 1.2. 비자발적 입원을 피하고 있는가? 그렇다면 비자발적 입원을 피하기 위해 어떤 것이 수행되는가?
>
> 1.3. 비자발적 입원 대비 자발적 입원의 비율은 어떠한가?
>
> 1.4. 근래 비자발적 입원의 빈도는 어떠한가? (예를 들어 지난 18개월 동안) 어떤 환경에서 이루어졌는가?
>
> 1.5. 비자발적 입원 환자에 대한 선택 사항은 무엇인가? 〔예를 들어 외래 치료, 통원 치료, 생활 지지 아파트, 부분입원(partial hospitalization) 등〕

2. 정신보건 시설의 출입은 다른 질병을 위한 여타 시설에 대한 출입과 같은 방식으로 관리되어야 한다.

> 정신보건 시설의 출입은 어떻게 관리되는가? 다음 사항에 대한 출입 관리에 차이가 있는가?
>
> a. 자발적 환자 / 비자발적 환자
>
> b. 보험 환자 / 비보험 환자
>
> c. 공공 기관에서 서비스를 제공받는 환자 / 민간 기관에서 서비스

를 제공받는 환자

   d. 범죄를 저지른 환자 / 일반 환자

   e. 폭력적 환자 / 비폭력적 환자

3. 비자발적 입원이 아닌 환자의 경우, 다음의 원칙 16에서 규정한 바와 같이 비자발적 환자로 구금되어야 할 기준에 속하지 않는 한 언제라도 정신보건 시설에서 퇴원할 권리를 가지며, 그러한 권리를 고지해주어야 한다.

   3.1. 모든 자발적 환자는 언제든지 정신보건 시설에서 퇴원할 자유가 있는가? 이러한 자유를 제한하는 규정은 무엇인가? 예를 들면, 시설에서 퇴원하려고 한다면 환자는 허가가 필요한가? 허가 요청은 일반적으로 승인되는가? 환자 스스로가 의학적 조언에 반하여 퇴원하려고 한다면 환자가 거쳐야 하는 절차는 무엇인가?

   3.2. 환자는 의학적 조언에 반하는 경우라 할지라도 허가를 요구하거나 퇴원을 요청할 권리를 고지받는가?

   3.3. 어떤 환경에서 환자가 정신보건 시설에서 퇴원할 자유가 제한되는가?

   3.4. 새로 입원한 환자는 입원 시 환영받는 느낌을 받는가?

   3.5. 그들은 시설의 주요 규칙에 대해 어떻게 고지받는가?

   3.6. 그들은 어떻게 자신의 권리를 고지받는가? 언제 자신의 권리를 고지받는가? 환자의 권리는 환자가 접근 가능하며 주목을 끄는 장소에 열거되고 게시되는가? (원칙 12의 1. 참조)

   3.7. 모든 의료진과 환자 당사자가 함께 퇴원 계획을 논의하는가?

   3.8. 환자가 여타 시설에 대해 문의할 때에는 언제든지,

    • 환자에게 주어지는 표준 정보 양식이 있는가?

• 그러한 정보 양식은 그 시설로 발송되는가?

3.9. 어떤 추후 조치가 취해지는가? 환자가 자신의 지역사회에서 이용 가능한 다른 보건 및 사회복지 서비스를 이용할 수 있게 되는가?

3.10. 약물 치료는 적절하게 계속되는가? 예를 들어 처방전이 전달되는가? 특히 약물 치료 기록과 같은 의무 기록이 전달되는가? 환자가 지역사회로 복귀한다고 가정할 때, 환자는 약을 얻을 수 있는 방법과 장소를 인지하고 있는가? 약을 전달하는 의료진과 그 약을 받는 시설은 직접 연결되는가? 그렇다면 만약의 경우에 이를 대체할 절차는 있는가?

비자발적 입원
involuntary admission

1. 어떤 사람을 정신보건 시설에 비자발적 환자로 입원시키거나, 자발적으로 정신보건 시설에 입원한 사람을 비자발적 환자로 계속 입원시킬 수 있는 경우는 다음에 한한다. 법에 의해 해당 목적에 대한 허가를 받은 자격 있는 정신보건 전문가가 앞의 원칙 4에 따라 해당 환자가 정신장애를 가지고 있다고 진단하며 다음과 같다고 판단할 경우이다.

(a) 정신장애로 인해 환자나 타인에게 직접적이고 절박한 위해가 발생할 가능성이 매우 높다고 보거나

(b) 정신장애가 심각하고 판단력이 손상된 사람의 경우, 해당 환자를 입원 및 계속 입원시키지 못한다면 환자의 상태가 심각하게 악화될 것으로 예상하거나, 이 원칙에 따른 정신보건 시설 입원으로만 가능한 적정 치료나 최소 제한적인 대안 치료를 할 수 없게 될 것이라고 판단할 경우

(b)항에 해당되는 경우에는 첫 번째 정신보건 전문가와 관계가 없는 다른 정신보건 전문가의 의견을 가능한 한 참조해야 한다. 이때 두 번째 정신보건 전문가가 동의하지 않는다면 비자발적 입원이나 계속 입원을 시켜서는 안 된다.

1.1. 환자의 비자발적 입원은 누가 결정하는가?

1.2. 비자발적 입원의 이유는 무엇인가?

1.3. 비자발적 입원이 인정되기 위해서는 두 번째 정신보건 전문가의 의견이 요구되는가?

만약 그렇다면,

- 누가 두 번째 정신보건 전문가를 선택하는가?
- 개별적인 정신상태검사(MSE)가 있는가?
- 두 가지 검사 결과가 수행되고 개별적으로 서류화되는가?
- 두 번째 정신보건 전문가는 첫 번째 전문가와 다른 시설 소속인가?
- 두 번째 정신보건 전문가는 환자의 모든 기록을 열람할 수 있는가? 또는 그러한 열람이 편견을 갖게 하지 않는가?

1.4. 지방정부법은 이러한 비자발적 입원을 촉진하는 방식으로 초안되었는가? 예를 들어 자발적 환자가 비자발적 환자로서 병원에 입원을 지속할 수 없다면 의학적 충고에 반하여 퇴원해야 하고, 그 후에 비자발적인 근거하에 재입원해야 한다. 실제 상황에서 처음에 환자를 입원시킬 원동력은 환자 상태에 대해 정당화되는지와 관계없이 비자발적인 근거하에 이루어져야 한다.

2. 비자발적인 입원이나 계속 입원은, 심사 기관의 입원·계속 입원 심사 계류 중에 관찰과 예비적 치료를 위해, 국내법에 정한 대로 단기간에 한해 실시되어야 한다. 입원의 근거를 즉시 환자에게 전해야 하며, 또한 입원 사실과 그 자세한 근거를 즉시 심사 기관과 환자의 개인 대리인이 있는 경우 대리인, 그리고 환자가 반대하지 않는 경우 환자의 가족에게 알려야 한다.

2.1. 환자는 얼마 동안 비자발적으로 입원되는가? 이러한 기간은 법률에 의해 결정되거나 제한되는가?

2.2. 환자는 자신의 입원 근거를 아는가?

2.3. 그 밖의 누구에게 비자발적 입원이 고지되는가? 이것에 대해 환자의 동의가 필요한가? 비자발적으로 입원되는 미성년자의 입원 절

차는 무엇인가? 부모나 후견인은 통상적으로 이에 대해 고지받는가?

3. 정신보건 시설의 경우, 국내법에 의한 해당 권한 기관이 지정한 시설에서만 비자발적 입원 환자를 수용할 수 있다.

3.1. 비자발적 환자를 수용하는 정신보건 시설은 해당 권한 기관이 지정했는가?

3.2. 정신보건 시설을 특별히 분류된 비자발적 환자를 수용하기에 적합하다고 지정할 수 있는 해당 권한 기관은 어디인가? 예를 들어 그 시설은 범죄를 저지른 환자를 수용하고 치료하기에 적절하게 갖춰진 곳으로 특별히 지정되었는가?

원칙 17

심사 기관
review body

1. 심사 기관은 국내법에 의해 설립된 사법 기관 및 기타 독립적인 공정한 기관으로서, 그 직무가 국내법에 의해 정해진 절차에 따라 운영되어야 한다. 심사 기관은 공식적인 결정을 내릴 때 자격을 갖춘 독립적인 정신보건 전문가 1인 이상의 조언을 참고해야 한다.

1.1. 정신보건 시설에서 비자발적 환자의 입원 또는 계속 입원을 심사하는 기관의 성격은 어떠한가?

1.2. 심사 기관의 구성은 어떠한가? 구성원은 임명되고 선출되며 고용되는가? 누구에게 고용되는가?

1.3. 심사 기관은 어떤 조언을 받는가? 누구에게서 받는가? 어떤 형식으로 받는가? 예를 들어 기록의 검토, 과거 기록, 독립적 증언?

1.4. 이러한 조언은 어떻게 적용되는가?

2. 앞의 원칙 16의 2항에 해당하는 비자발적 환자의 입원이나 계속 입원 결정에 대한 심사 기관의 최초 심사는 해당 결정이 내려진 직후 가능한 한 빨리 이루어져야 하며, 국내법에 의해 규정된 대로 간단하고 신속한 절차에 따라 수행되어야 한다.

개인의 입원 또는 계속 입원이 결정된 후 최초 심사가 연기되고 있는가?

3. 심사 기관은 국내법에 의해 규정된 대로 적당한 기간마다 주기적으로 비자
발적 환자의 경우를 심사해야 한다.

심사 기관은 특별히 지정된 기간 안에 결정을 내려야 하는가? 그렇다
면 기간은 얼마 동안인가? 그렇지 않다면 심사 기관이 결정을 내리는
데 필요한 일반적인 기간은 어느 정도인가?

4. 비자발적 환자는 국내법에 의해 규정된 대로 적당한 기간을 두고 심사
기관에 퇴원이나 자발적 상태로의 전환을 신청할 수 있다.

환자는 얼마 동안의 간격을 두고 심사 기관에 퇴원이나 자발적 상태로
의 전환을 요청할 수 있는가?

5. 개개의 심사에서 심사 기관은 앞의 원칙 16의 1항에 제시된 비자발적 입원
기준에 여전히 속하는지를 고려해야 하며, 그렇지 않은 경우 환자는 비자발적
상태를 벗어나 퇴원할 수 있어야 한다.

어떤 조건에서 환자가 퇴원되는가?

6. 담당 정신보건 전문가는 환자가 비자발적 환자로서 계속 입원해야 하는
요건에 더 이상 해당되지 않는다고 판단한 경우, 언제라도 퇴원 지시를 내려야
한다.

6.1. 정신보건 전문가는 국내법에 의해 비자발적 환자로서 입원을 해
야 하는 요건에 더 이상 해당되지 않는다고 판단한 경우, 환자의 비자

발적 상태에서 자발적 상태로의 전환을 요구하는가?

6.2. 비자발적 입원의 요건에 더 이상 해당되지 않을 경우, 정신보건 의료 전문가는 지방정부법에 따라 환자를 비자발적 상태에서 자발적 상태로 전환하는 것을 허용하는가?

7. 환자나 환자의 개인 대리인 또는 기타 이해관계인은 정신보건 시설 입원이나 계속 입원 결정에 대해 상급법원에 항소할 권리를 가져야 한다.

7.1. 환자나 환자의 후견인은 환자의 정신보건 시설 입원 또는 계속 입원 결정에 대해 항소할 권리를 가지는가?

절차상의 보호조치
procedural safeguards

1. 환자는 이의 제기 절차나 항소 시 대변인은 물론이고 자신을 대리할 대리인을 선택해 선임할 권리를 가져야 한다. 환자 자신이 그러한 서비스를 확보하지 않았을 경우, 환자가 지불할 여력이 없다면 무료로 대리인을 확보할 수 있어야 한다.

> 1.1. 이의 제기 절차나 항소 시 환자가 어떻게 대변되는가?
>
> 1.2. 이러한 대변 과정에 대해 경제적으로 어떻게 보상하는가?

2. 또한 환자는 필요한 경우 통역 서비스를 받을 권리를 가져야 한다. 통역 서비스가 필요지만 환자 스스로 이를 확보하지 않은 경우, 환자에게 지불 여력이 없다면 무료로 제공되어야 한다.

> 2.1. 환자가 법원의 공용어를 자유자재로 구사하지 못하는 경우, 환자는 필요하다면 무료로 통역 서비스를 제공받을 수 있는가?

3. 환자와 환자의 대리인은 심리 시에 독립적인 정신보건 보고서와 기타 보고서, 관련된 구두·서면·기타 증거자료를 요청하고 제시할 수 있다.

> 3.1. 환자나 환자의 대리인은 독립적인 정신보건 보고서와 기타 보고서, 관련된 구두·서면·기타 증거자료를 요구할 권리가 있는가? 이러

한 독립적인 사정에 대해 누가 재정을 지원하는가?

4. 환자 기록 및 제출되는 기타 보고서와 자료들은, 환자에게 해당 자료가 공개될 경우 환자의 건강에 심각한 위해가 초래되거나 다른 이의 안전에 위험을 초래할 것으로 판정되는 특별한 경우를 제외하고, 환자와 그 대리인에게 사본을 전달해야 한다. 환자에게 전달하지 않은 기록은, 국내법 규정이 있다면 그에 따라, 비밀리에 전달이 가능한 경우 환자의 개인 대리인과 대리인에게 전달해야 한다. 기록 중 환자에게 알리지 않은 부분이 있는 경우에는 환자나 환자의 대리인에게 그 사실과 이유를 고지해야 하며, 이는 법원의 심사를 거쳐야 한다.

4.1. 환자 기록(그리고 제출되는 기타 보고서 및 자료)은 환자와 환자의 대리인에게 전달되는가?

4.2. 그렇지 않다면 왜 전달되지 않는가?

4.3. 그렇다면 언제 전달되는가? 그 자료는 적절한 심사 기회를 제공하는 심리가 시작되기 전, 충분한 시간적 여유를 두고 전달되는가?

4.4. 환자에게 전달되지 않고 환자의 개인 대리인과 대리인에게 전달된 자료가 있는가? 그렇다면 어떤 사정으로 그러한가?

4.5. 기록이나 그 일부를 알려주지 않을 경우, 환자는 이를 고지받는가?

4.6. 그 밖에 누가 고지받는가?

4.7. 이렇게 기록을 알려주지 않는 이유는 무엇인가?

4.8. 이렇게 기록을 알려주지 않을 경우 법원의 심사가 이루어지는가?

5. 환자와 환자의 개인 대리인 및 대리인은 심리에 직접 출석해 참여하고 발언할 수 있는 권리를 가져야 한다.

5.1. 환자는 의미 있는 방법으로 심리에 직접 출석해 참여하고 발언할 수 있는 권리를 가지는가?

5.2. 이러한 권리를 또 누가 가지는가?

5.3. 환자는 이러한 심리에서 증언할 권리를 가지는가?

6. 환자나 환자의 개인 대리인 및 대리인이 심리에 특정인의 출석을 요청할 경우에는, 그 사람의 출석이 환자의 건강에 심각한 위해를 초래하거나 다른 이의 안전에 위험을 초래할 수 있다고 판정된 경우가 아닌 한 허용해야 한다.

6.1. 누가 심리에 출석할 수 있는가?

6.2. 누가 그 사람의 심리 출석을 결정하는가?

6.3. 환자가 심리에 특정인의 출석을 요청하는 것이 지켜지는가?

6.4. 또 누가 그러한 요청을 할 자격이 있으며 그 요청은 받아들여지는가? 그렇지 않다면 왜 그러한가?

7. 심리나 그 과정이 공개적으로 이루어져야 할지 비밀리에 이루어져야 할지와 공개적으로 보도되어도 좋을지에 대한 결정을 내릴 때는 반드시 환자 자신의 바람과 환자 및 다른 사람들의 사생활 존중을 위한 필요성, 환자의 건강에 대한 심각한 위해를 막거나 다른 이들의 안전에 대한 위험을 피하기 위한 요건을 충분히 고려해야 한다.

7.1. 심리에서 환자의 권리는 무엇인가? 심리는 공식적인가, 비공식적인가?

7.2. 이 문제는 누가 결정하는가?

7.3. 환자의 사생활은 존중되며 비밀 보장은 유지되는가?

7.4. 타인의 사생활은 존중되는가?

7.5. 개인 대리인과 대리인의 권리는 무엇인가?

7.6. 환자의 대리인은 이러한 권리를 어떻게 고지받는가?

8. 심리를 통한 결정과 그에 대한 이유는 서면으로 작성되어야 하며, 그 사본을 환자와 환자의 개인 대리인 및 대리인에게 전해야 한다. 결정 사항을 전체 또는 부분적으로 공개 발표해야 할지에 대한 결정을 내릴 때는, 환자 자신의 바람과 환자 및 다른 사람들의 사생활 존중을 위한 필요성, 환자의 건강에 대한 심각한 위해를 막거나 다른 이들의 안전에 대한 위험을 피하기 위한 요건을 충분히 고려해야 한다.

8.1. 심리에서 결정된 사항은 어떤 형식으로 표현되는가?

8.2. 그러한 결정이 내려진 이유는 무엇인가?

8.3. 누가 결정 사항의 공개를 결정하는가?

8.4. 환자는 그 결정 사항의 사본을 받는가?

8.5. 환자의 위협을 예방하기 위해 무엇이 행해지는가?

8.6. 환자가 편하게 느끼도록 무엇이 행해지는가?

정보 열람
access to information

1. 환자(이 원칙에서는 과거에 환자였던 사람도 포함함)는 정신보건 시설에서 관리하는 자신의 건강 및 개인 기록에서 자신과 관련된 정보를 열람할 수 있는 권리를 가져야 한다. 이 권리는 환자 자신의 건강에 대한 심각한 위해를 예방하고 다른 사람의 안전을 위험에 빠뜨리지 않기 위한 목적으로 제한을 받을 수도 있다. 이와 같이 환자에게 제한된 정보가 있는 경우에는 국내법 규정이 있다면 그에 따라, 환자의 개인 대리인 및 대리인에게 비밀리에 전달이 가능하다면 그렇게 해야 한다. 환자에게 제한된 정보가 있는 경우에는 환자나 환자의 대리인에게 그 사실과 이유를 고지해야 하며, 이는 법원의 심사를 거쳐야 한다.

  1.1. 환자는 자신의 의무 기록을 요청하는 대로 열람할 수 있는가?
  1.2. 그렇지 않다면 왜 이러한 정보를 알리지 않는가?
  1.3. 정보가 환자에게 알려지지 않는다면 누가 이를 고지받을 것인가?
  1.4. 환자에게 전달되지 않는다면 누구에게 그러한 정보가 전달되는가?
  1.5. 환자는 정신보건 전문가와 함께 자신의 기록을 열람하는가, 아니면 단독으로 열람하는가?
  1.6. 정보가 환자에게 알려지지 않는다면 어떤 법적 절차를 따르는가?

2. 환자나 환자의 개인 대리인 및 대리인에 의한 서면 설명은 요청이 있을 경우 환자의 자료에 포함해야 한다.

2.1. 환자의 기록에는 어떤 정보가 포함되는가?

2.2. 정보는 읽기 쉬운 형식으로 기록되며 비밀이 충분히 보장되는가?

2.3. 환자나 환자의 개인 대리인은, 그가 기존의 기록들을 바꾸지 않는 한, 의견을 추가하거나 기타 자료를 자신의 기록에 첨부할 수 있는가?

범죄 피의자
criminal offenders

1. 이 원칙은 형사 범죄자로 징역 중이거나 형사 절차나 수사 대상으로 유치 중인 사람으로서 정신장애를 가지고 있거나 그러한 질환이 의심되는 것으로 판단되는 사람에게 적용된다.

> 1.1. 누가 범죄 피의자로 여겨지는가?
> 1.2. 정신이상 때문에 무죄판결을 받은(Not Guilty by Reason of Insanity: NGRI) 경우가 있는가?
> 1.3. 그렇다면 NGRI 판정을 받은 사람을 위한 일정한 절차가 있는가?
> 1.4. 정신장애인이 보석금을 내고 석방되는 것은 어떠한가? 그들이 자유로운 상태로 치료받도록 요구되는가? 이러한 치료가 어떻게 입증되는가? 치료가 뒤따르도록 하는 적절한 가석방 제도가 있는가?

2. 이와 같은 사람은 앞의 원칙 1에서 설명하는 바와 같이 최상의 정신보건 의료를 받아야 한다. 주어진 상황에서 꼭 필요한 경우 제한적인 수정과 예외는 있을 수 있으나, 가능한 한 최대한 이 UN 원칙을 적용해야 한다. 제한적인 수정과 예외 사항들도 원칙 1의 5항에 명기된 협정에 따른 권리를 침해할 수는 없다.

> 2.1. 감옥 제도에서 수감자들의 보건의료 특성은 어떠한가?
> 2.2. 수감자들에게 보건의료는 보장되는가?

2.3. 각 개별 감옥 내에 병원 구역이 있는가?

2.4. 수감자들에게 정신보건 의료는 보장되는가?

2.5. 정신장애 수감자들이 치료받을 수 있는 특정한 법의학적 병원이 근처에 있는가?

2.6. 정신장애 수감자들은 일반 수감자들과 함께 수감되는가 아니면 개별적·반개별적 공간 또는 감옥의 병원 구역 내에 수감되는가?

3. 이러한 사람들의 경우, 법원이나 기타 정당한 권한 기관이 합당하고 독립적인 의학적 조언을 근거로 정신보건 시설 입원을 명할 권한을 갖도록 국내법에 의해 규정할 수 있다.

3.1. 수감자는 정신보건 시설에 입원할 수 있는가?

3.2. 그렇다면 어느 시설에, 어떤 목적을 위해 입원하는가?

  a. 법적 행위능력 회복을 위해 입원하는가? 심리 전 또는 후에 입원하는가?

  b. 입원은 형의 일부인가? 정신보건 시설에서 형의 전부 또는 일부를 복역하는가?

3.3. 만약 3.1.의 대답이 '예'일 경우, 수감자는 누구에 의해 입원되는가?

3.4. 어떠한 경우에도 치료에 대한 동의를 고지받을 수감자의 권리는 존중되는가? 법정에 서기 위해서 법적 행위능력의 회복을 고려하여 치료의 자발성은 어떻게 보호되는가? 예를 들어 수감자가 법적 행위능력은 갖추지 못했으나 회복될 가능성이 있는 경우, 그는 능력을 회복시킬 것으로 여겨지는 치료를 거부하는가?

4. 정신장애를 가진 것으로 판정된 수감자의 치료는 반드시 앞의 원칙 11에

따라야 한다.

4.1. 특히 개인의 강박과 같은 사생활 제한과 관련해, 정신장애를 가진 수감자 개인의 고결성에 관한 특정 보호 장치는 무엇인가?

4.2. 교도관과 감옥의 직원은 정신장애의 기본 증상을 인지하도록 교육받는가?

4.3. 교도관과 감옥의 직원은 정신장애를 가진 사람들의 필요에 민감하게 대처하도록 교육받는가?

4.4. 지역의 감옥 체계에서 정신장애인이 차지하는 비율이 지나치게 높은가? 정신장애의 동반 질환의 양상이 다른 장소에 비해 불균형을 보이는가? 즉, 정신장애가 사실상 유죄로 취급받는가?

4.5. 보건의료 제도 대신 감옥 제도가 정신장애인의 주거나 보호 목적으로 사용되는가?

이의 제기
complaints

모든 환자 및 과거에 환자였던 사람에게는 국내법에 규정된 절차에 따라 이의를 제기할 수 있는 권리가 주어져야 한다.

1. 정신보건 체계에서 환자가 자신의 경험에 대해 이의를 제기하는데 어떠한 절차가 존재하는가?

2. 환자와 시설에서 제기하는 이의를 처리하는 이용 가능한 서면으로 된 절차가 있는가?

3. 이의의 제기, 조사, 해결은 보장되는가?

4. 어떤 수준의 권한 기관이 이러한 이의를 처리하는가?

5. 이의를 제기하는 환자를 보복으로부터 보호하기 위해 사례를 검토하는 추적 절차가 있는가?

감시와 구제
monitoring and remedies

정부는 이 UN 원칙의 준수를 촉구하기 위해, 정신보건 시설 조사, 불만 사항의 접수·조사·해결, 전문인의 위법 행위나 환자 권리의 침해에 대한 징계 및 사법 절차 제도를 위한 적법한 절차와 기구를 마련하여 시행하도록 해야 한다.

1. 정부는 이 원칙의 준수를 촉구하기 위해 무엇을 하는가?

2. 정신보건 시설에 대한 조사 계획이 있는가?

3. 환자의 권리 침해 또는 상습적인 위법 행위에 대비해 어떠한 대응 절차가 있는가?

4. 이 원칙의 준수는 인가 또는 전문인 자격 부여에 영향을 미치는가?

5. 준수하지 않는 결과는 무엇인가? 예를 들면 시설이 폐쇄되거나, 제3자에 의한 보상이 인정되지 않거나 보호관찰하에 운영되는가?

6. 행정적인 처벌뿐만 아니라 형사상의 처벌이 있는가? 이것들은 강행되는가?

7. 정신장애인을 학대하거나 소홀히 대한 개인이 쉽게 타국 또는 타

지역으로 이주하거나 다른 면허를 취득해 개업하지 못하도록 국내 및 국제 기록이 유지되고 상호 참조되는가?

실행
implementation

1. 정부는 적절한 입법적·사법적·행정적·교육적·기타 조치들을 통해 이 UN 원칙을 실행해야 하며, 이를 주기적으로 심사해야 한다.

> 1.1. 이 UN 원칙을 실행하기 위해 어떠한 조치(입법적·사법적·행정적·교육적·기타 조치)가 취해지는가?
>
> 1.2. 이 조치는 얼마나 자주 심사되는가?
>
> 1.3. 이 UN 원칙의 실행과 이러한 실행이 충분히 지속되는 것을 보장하기 위한 전략이 있는가?
>
> 1.4. 정신보건은 어떻게 증진되는가?
>
> 1.5. 정신보건 프로그램의 준비와 지속을 위해 누가 참여하는가?
>
> 1.6. 정신보건 의료의 질을 향상시키고 유지하는 목적을 가진 특정한 정부 기구가 있는가?

2. 정부는 적절하고 적극적인 수단을 동원하여 이 UN 원칙을 널리 알려야 한다.

> 2.1. 이 UN 원칙은 어떻게 널리 보급되는가?
>
> 2.2. 홍보 원칙은 있는가?
>
> 2.3. 이 UN 원칙의 내용은 일반인에게도 알려져 있는가?
>
> 2.4. 이 UN 원칙의 내용은 각 지역의 언어로 알려져 있는가?

정신보건 시설에 대한 원칙의 적용 범위
scope of principles relating to mental health facilities

이 UN 원칙은 정신보건 시설에 입원한 모든 이에게 적용된다.

1. 이 UN 원칙은 정신보건 시설에 입원한 모든 이에게 적용되는가?

2. 그렇지 않다면 어떤 유형의 환자에게 언제, 어떤 사정에서, 얼마나 오랫동안 적용될 수 없는가?

기존 권리의 구제

saving of existing rights

이 UN 원칙에서 인정하지 않고 있거나 또는 더 좁은 범위로 인정하고 있다는 이유로, 적용 가능한 국제 및 국내법에서 인정하고 있는 권리 등 환자의 기존 권리가 제한되거나 훼손되어서는 안 된다.

1. 이 UN 원칙은 정신장애인 권리의 견지에서 충족되는 최소한의 기준 또는 출발점으로 여겨지는가, 아니면 최고 한도로 여겨지는가?

2. 이 원칙의 실행이 정신장애인의 권리와 치료를 제한·금지하거나 기준을 낮추는 방식으로 사용되는가?

제 2부

점검표
Checklist

점검표

	예	아니오
1. 정신장애인은 자신의 시민권 및 경제적·문화적 권리를 행사할 수 있습니까? 예를 들어,		
1.1. 결혼할 권리		
1.2. 재산권		
1.3. 투표권		
1.4. 자녀를 가지며 양육할 수 있는 권리		
1.5. 자신의 의료 기록을 열람할 권리		
1.6. 잔인하고 비인간적이거나 낮은 수준의 치료 또는 처벌로부터 자유로울 권리		
2. 정신장애인의 차별을 금지하는 법률이 있습니까? 만약 그렇다면 구체적으로 설명하시오.		
3. 정신보건 의료를 관리하는 법률이 있습니까? 만약 그렇다면 구체적으로 설명하시오.		
4. 환자의 참여를 규정하는 법률이 있습니까? (치료 그리고/또는 입원에 대한) 만약 그렇다면 구체적으로 설명하시오.		
5. 정신보건 의료의 질을 유지하고 향상시키는 것을 담당하는 전문 정부 기관이 있습니까? 만약 그렇다면 구체적으로 설명하시오.		
6. 미성년 정신장애인에 대한 교육을 제공합니까?		
7. 정신장애를 판단하는 기준이 있습니까? (예를 들어 ICD, DSM) 만약 그렇다면 구체적으로 설명하시오.		

8. 신체장애인의 경우에 필적하는, 정신장애인을 위한 의료 기준이 있습니까?		
9. 다른 보건 시설에 필적하는, 정신보건 시설을 위한 자원(인력, 재정, 물적 자원)이 있습니까?		
10. 환자는 치료 시작 전에 항상 고지된 동의를 요청받습니까?		
11. 허용되는 강박의 유형이 있습니까? 허용되지 않는 강박의 유형이 있습니까? 만약 그렇다면 구체적으로 설명하시오.		
12. 정신장애에 대한 약물 요법의 사용은 국제적으로 인증된 지침을 따릅니까? 만약 그렇다면 구체적으로 설명하시오.		
13. 정신장애의 치료를 위해 널리 이용 가능한(모든 환자에게 도보로 한 시간 거리 내에) 필수 의약품이 있습니까? 구체적으로 설명하시오.		
14. 비밀을 보장하기 위해 운영되는 제도가 있습니까?		
15. 환자가 요구하는 대로 자신의 의료 기록을 열람할 수 있습니까?		
16. 정신보건 시설에서 치료받는 환자는 항상 자신의 권리를 고지받습니까?		
17. 자발적 입원 절차가 있습니까?		
18. 비자발적 입원에 제한 기간이 있습니까? 만약 그렇다면 구체적으로 설명하시오.		
19. 환자들은 비자발적 입원 결정에 대해 이의를 제기할 권리가 있습니까? 만약 그렇다면 구체적으로 설명하시오.		

20. 불만을 표현할 수 있는 절차가 있거나 이의를 제기할 환경에서 환자가 주장을 펼 수 있습니까? 만약 그렇다면 구체적으로 설명하시오.		
21. 정신장애인의 필요를 충족하는 주거 형태가 있습니까? (시설이나 지역사회 모두에서) 만약 그렇다면 구체적으로 설명하시오.		
22. 정신사회적 재활을 위해 취해지는 특정한 프로그램이나 조치가 있습니까? 만약 그렇다면 구체적으로 설명하시오.		
23. 감옥이나 교도소가 정신장애인을 수용하는 곳으로 사용됩니까?		
24. 정신장애인 수감자를 위한 전문 법의학 병원이 있습니까?		
25. 정신보건 의료가 수감자에게도 보장됩니까?		
26. 통상적으로 환자가 치료받는 곳은 집으로부터 어느 정도의 거리에 있습니까?		
27. 정신장애 환자의 평균 입원 기간은 얼마 동안입니까?		
28. 비자발적 입원에 비해 자발적 입원의 비율은 얼마입니까?		
29. 비자발적 입원 시 몇 명의 서명(누구의 서명)이 필요합니까?		
30. 어느 권한 기관이 비자발적 입원을 심사합니까?		

부록 1

인권 관련 국제 선언문

세계인권선언

Universal Declaration of Human Rights*

1948년 12월 10일 국제연합 총회에서 채택

인류 가족 모든 구성원의 고유한 존엄성과 평등하고 양도할 수 없는 권리를 인정하는 것이 세계의 자유, 정의, 평화의 기초가 됨을 인정하며,

인권에 대한 무시와 경멸은 인류의 양심을 짓밟는 야만적 행위를 초래하였으며, 인류가 언론의 자유, 신념의 자유, 공포와 궁핍으로부터의 자유를 향유하는 세계의 도래가 모든 사람들의 지고한 열망으로 천명되었으며,

사람들이 폭정과 억압에 대항하는 마지막 수단으로서 반란에 호소하도록 강요받지 않으려면, 인권이 법에 의한 지배에 의하여 보호되어야 함이 필수적이며,

국가 간의 친선 관계의 발전을 촉진하는 것이 긴요하며,

국제연합의 여러 국민들은 그 헌장에서 기본적 인권, 인간의 존엄과 가치, 남녀의 동등한 권리에 대한 신념을 재확인하였으며, 더욱 폭넓은 자유 속에서 사회적 진보와 생활수준의 개선을 촉진할 것을 다짐하였으며,

회원국들은 국제연합과 협력하여 인권과 기본적 자유에 대한 보편적 존중과 준수의 증진을 달성할 것을 서약하였으며,

이러한 권리와 자유에 대한 공통의 이해가 이 서약의 이행을 위하여

---

* 유네스코 한국위원회 국제인권조약집(http://www.unesco.or.kr/hrtreaty/)

가장 중요하므로,

따라서 국제연합 총회는 모든 개인과 사회의 각 기관은 세계인권선언을 항상 마음속에 간직한 채, 교육과 학습을 통하여 이러한 권리와 자유에 대한 존중을 신장시키기 위하여 노력하고, 점진적인 국내적 그리고 국제적 조치를 통하여 회원국 국민 및 회원국 관할하의 영토의 국민들 양자 모두에게 권리와 자유의 보편적이고 효과적인 인정과 준수를 보장하기 위하여 힘쓰도록, 모든 국민들과 국가에 대한 공통의 기준으로서 본 세계인권선언을 선포한다.

제1조 모든 사람은 태어날 때부터 자유롭고, 존엄성과 권리에서 평등하다. 사람은 이성과 양심을 부여받았으며 서로 형제애의 정신으로 대하여야 한다.

제2조 모든 사람은 인종, 피부색, 성, 언어, 종교, 정치적 또는 그 밖의 견해, 민족적 또는 사회적 출신, 재산, 출생, 기타의 지위 등에 따른 어떠한 종류의 차별도 없이, 이 선언에 제시된 모든 권리와 자유를 누릴 자격이 있다. 나아가 개인이 속한 나라나 영역이 독립국이든 신탁통치 지역이든, 비자치 지역이든 또는 그 밖의 다른 주권상의 제한을 받고 있는 지역이든, 그 나라나 영역의 정치적·사법적·국제적 지위를 근거로 차별이 행하여져서는 아니 된다.

제3조 모든 사람은 생명권과 신체의 자유와 안전을 누릴 권리가 있다.

제4조 어느 누구도 노예나 예속 상태에 놓이지 아니한다. 모든 형태의

노예제도 및 노예 매매는 금지된다.

제5조 어느 누구도 고문, 또는 잔혹하거나 비인도적이거나 모욕적인 취급 혹은 형벌을 받지 아니한다.

제6조 모든 사람은 어디에서나 법 앞에 인간으로서 인정받을 권리를 가진다.

제7조 모든 사람은 법 앞에 평등하고, 어떠한 차별도 없이 법의 평등한 보호를 받을 권리를 가진다. 모든 사람은 이 선언을 위반하는 어떠한 차별에 대하여도, 또한 어떠한 차별의 선동에 대하여도 평등한 보호를 받을 권리를 가진다.

제8조 모든 사람은 헌법 또는 법률이 부여하는 기본권을 침해하는 행위에 대하여 담당 국가 법원에 의하여 실효성 있는 구제를 받을 권리를 가진다.

제9조 어느 누구도 자의적인 체포, 구금 또는 추방을 당하지 아니한다.

제10조 모든 사람은 자신의 권리와 의무, 그리고 자신에 대한 형사상의 혐의를 결정함에 있어서, 독립적이고 편견 없는 법정에서 공정하고도 공개적인 심문을 전적으로 평등하게 받을 권리를 가진다.

제11조 1. 형사 범죄로 소추당한 모든 사람은 자신의 변호에 필요한 모든 장치를 갖춘 공개된 재판에서 법률에 따라 유죄로 입증될

때까지 무죄로 추정받을 권리를 가진다.

  2. 어느 누구도 행위 시의 국내법 또는 국제법상으로 범죄를 구
    성하지 아니하는 작위 또는 부작위를 이유로 유죄로 되지 아
    니한다. 또한 범죄가 행하여진 때에 적용될 수 있는 형벌보다
    무거운 형벌이 부과되지 아니한다.

제12조 어느 누구도 자신의 사생활, 가정, 주거 또는 통신에 대하여 자의
    적인 간섭을 받지 않으며, 자신의 명예와 신용에 대하여 공격을
    받지 아니한다. 모든 사람은 그러한 간섭과 공격에 대하여 법률
    의 보호를 받을 권리를 가진다.

제13조 1. 모든 사람은 각국의 영역 내에서 이전과 거주의 자유에 관한
      권리를 가진다.

     2. 모든 사람은 자국을 포함한 어떤 나라로부터도 출국할 권리
      가 있으며, 또한 자국으로 돌아올 권리를 가진다.

제14조 1. 모든 사람은 박해를 피하여 타국에서 피난처를 구하고 보호
      를 받을 권리를 가진다.

     2. 이 권리는 비정치적인 범죄 또는 국제연합의 목적과 원칙에
      반하는 행위만으로 인하여 제기된 소추의 경우에는 활용될
      수 없다.

제15조 1. 모든 사람은 국적을 가질 권리를 가진다.

     2. 어느 누구도 자의적으로 자신의 국적을 박탈당하거나 그의
      국적을 바꿀 권리를 부인당하지 아니한다.

제16조 1. 성년에 이른 남녀는 인종, 국적 또는 종교에 따른 어떠한 제한도 받지 않고 혼인하여 가정을 이룰 권리를 가진다. 이들은 혼인 기간 중 또는 이혼 시에 혼인에 관하여 동등한 권리를 가진다.

2. 결혼은 양 당사자의 자유롭고도 완전한 합의에 의하여만 성립된다.

3. 가정은 사회의 자연적이며 기초적인 구성단위이며, 사회와 국가의 보호를 받을 권리가 있다.

제17조 1. 모든 사람은 단독으로는 물론이고 타인과 공동으로 자신의 재산을 소유할 권리를 가진다.

2. 어느 누구도 자신의 재산을 자의적으로 박탈당하지 아니한다.

제18조 모든 사람은 사상, 양심 및 종교의 자유에 대한 권리를 가진다. 이러한 권리는 자신의 종교 또는 신념을 바꿀 자유와 선교, 행사, 예배, 의식에서 단독으로 또는 다른 사람과 공동으로, 공적으로 또는 사적으로 자신의 종교나 신념을 표명하는 자유를 포함한다.

제19조 모든 사람은 의견과 표현의 자유에 관한 권리를 가진다. 이 권리는 간섭받지 않고 의견을 가질 자유와 모든 매체를 통하여 국경에 관계없이 정보와 사상을 추구하고, 접수하고, 전달하는 자유를 포함한다.

제20조 1. 모든 사람은 평화적 집회와 결사의 자유에 관한 권리를 가진다.

2. 어느 누구도 어떤 결사에 참여할 것을 강요받지 아니한다.

제21조 1. 모든 사람은 직접 또는 자유롭게 선출된 대표를 통하여 자국
        의 통치에 참여할 권리를 가진다.
       2. 모든 사람은 자국의 공무에 취임할 동등한 권리를 가진다.
       3. 국민의 의사는 정부의 권위의 기초가 된다. 이 의사는 보통
        및 평등 선거권에 의거하며, 비밀투표 또는 이와 동등한 자유
        로운 투표 절차에 따라 실시되는 정기적이고 진정한 선거를
        통하여 표현된다.

제22조 모든 사람은 사회의 일원으로서 사회보장제도에 관한 권리를
       가지며, 국가적 노력과 국제적 협력을 통하여, 그리고 각국의
       조직과 자원에 따라 자신의 존엄성과 인격의 자유로운 발전을
       위하여 불가결한 경제적·사회적·문화적 권리를 실현할 수 있는
       권리를 가진다.

제23조 1. 모든 사람은 근로의 권리, 자유로운 직업 선택권, 공정하고
        유리한 근로조건에 관한 권리 및 실업으로부터 보호받을 권
        리를 가진다.
       2. 모든 사람은 어떠한 차별도 받지 않고 동일한 노동에 대하여
        동등한 보수를 받을 권리를 가진다.
       3. 모든 근로자는 자신과 가족에게 인간적 존엄에 합당한 생활을
        보장하여 주며, 필요할 경우 다른 사회적 보호의 수단에 의하
        여 보완되는, 정당하고 유리한 보수를 받을 권리를 가진다.
       4. 모든 사람은 자신의 이익을 보호하기 위하여 노동조합을 결
        성하고 가입할 권리를 가진다.

제24조 모든 사람은 근로시간의 합리적 제한과 정기적인 유급휴가를 포함한 휴식과 여가에 관한 권리를 가진다.

제25조 1. 모든 사람은 식량, 의복, 주택, 의료, 필수적인 사회복지를 포함하여 자신과 가족의 건강과 안녕에 적합한 생활수준을 누릴 권리를 가지며, 실업, 질병, 불구, 배우자와의 사별, 노령, 그 밖의 자신이 통제할 수 없는 상황에서의 생계 결핍의 경우 사회보장을 누릴 권리를 가진다.

2. 모자는 특별한 보살핌과 도움을 받을 권리를 가진다. 모든 어린이는 부모의 혼인 여부에 관계없이 동등한 사회적 보호를 받아야 한다.

제26조 1. 모든 사람은 교육을 받을 권리를 가진다. 교육은 최소한 초등 기초 단계에서는 무상이어야 한다. 초등교육은 의무적이어야 한다. 기술교육과 직업교육은 일반적으로 이용할 수 있어야 하며, 고등교육도 모든 사람에게 능력에 따라 평등하게 개방되어야 한다.

2. 교육은 인격의 완전한 발전과 인권 및 기본적 자유에 대한 존중을 강화하는 것을 목표로 하여야 한다. 교육은 모든 국가들과 인종적 또는 종교적 집단 간의 이해, 관용 및 친선을 증진시키고 평화를 유지하기 위한 국제연합의 활동을 촉진시켜야 한다.

3. 부모는 자녀에게 제공되는 교육의 종류를 선택할 우선권을 가진다.

제27조 1. 모든 사람은 공동체의 문화생활에 자유롭게 참여하고, 예술을 감상하며, 과학의 진보와 그 혜택을 향유할 권리를 가진다.
2. 모든 사람은 자신이 창조한 모든 과학적·문학적·예술적 창작물에서 생기는 정신적·물질적 이익을 보호받을 권리를 가진다.

제28조 모든 사람은 이 선언에 제시된 권리와 자유가 완전히 실현될 수 있는 사회적·국제적 질서에 대한 권리를 가진다.

제29조 1. 모든 사람은 그 안에서만 자신의 인격을 자유롭고 완전하게 발전시킬 수 있는 공동체에 대하여 의무를 부담한다.
2. 모든 사람은 자신의 권리와 자유를 행사할 때, 타인의 권리와 자유에 대한 적절한 인정과 존중을 보장하고, 민주 사회의 도덕, 공공질서, 일반의 복지를 위하여 정당한 필요를 충족시키기 위한 목적에서만 법률에 규정된 제한을 받는다.
3. 이러한 권리와 자유는 어떤 경우에도 국제연합의 목적과 원칙에 반하여 행사될 수 없다.

제30조 이 선언의 그 어떠한 조항도 특정 국가, 집단 또는 개인이 이 선언에 규정된 어떠한 권리와 자유를 파괴할 목적의 활동에 종사할 수 있다거나, 또는 그와 같은 행위를 할 어떠한 권리를 가지는 것으로 해석하여서는 아니 된다.

장애인 권리선언

Declaration on the Rights of Disabled Persons

1975년 12월 9일 유엔 총회 결의문 3447(XXX)에 의하여 선언됨

총회는,

유엔 회원국들이 유엔 헌장에 의거하여 더 높은 생활수준과 완전고용, 경제적·사회적 진보 및 발전을 촉진시키기 위하여 유엔 기구와 상호 협력하여 공동의 또는 개별적 조치를 취하겠다는 협약에 유념하며,

인간의 권리 및 근본적 자유와 평화의 원리에 입각하여 유엔 헌장에서 표명하였던 인간의 존엄과 가치, 사회정의의 신념을 재확인하며,

「세계인권선언」, 「국제인권규약」, 「아동의 권리선언」, 「정신지체인 권리선언」의 여러 원칙들과 국제노동기구(ILO), 국제연합교육과학문화기구(UNESCO), 세계보건기구(WHO), 국제연합아동기금(UN Children's Fund) 및 기타 관련 기구의 규약, 협약, 권고 및 결의에서 사회 진보를 목적으로 이미 설정되었던 기준을 상기하며,

1975년 5월 6일, 장애 예방 및 장애인의 재활에 관한 경제사회이사회 결의문 1921(LVIII)을 회고하며,

「사회 진보와 발전에 관한 선언」이 심신장애인의 권리 보호와 재활 및 복지 확보의 필요성을 제창하였던 사실을 강조하며,

장애인이 다양한 활동 분야에서 자신의 능력을 발휘할 수 있도록 지원하고, 가능한 한 그들이 정상적인 생활로 통합될 수 있도록 촉진하여 심신장애 예방의 필요성이 있음을 유의하며,

일부 국가는 현재의 발전 단계에서 이러한 목적을 위하여 매우 제한된 노력밖에 기울일 수 없다는 사실을 인식하며,

본 「장애인 권리선언」을 선언하며, 다음과 같은 권리를 보호하기 위하여 공통적 기반과 준거 틀로 사용될 수 있도록 국내 및 국제적 행동을 촉구한다.

1. '장애인'은 신체적 또는 정신적 능력 면에서 선천적이나 후천적 결함으로 인하여 정상적인 개인 또는 사회생활을 스스로는 완전히 또는 부분적으로 영위할 수 없는 사람을 의미한다.

2. 장애인은 이 선언에 제시된 모든 권리를 향유할 수 있어야 한다. 이 권리는 예외 없이 주어지고, 인종, 피부색, 성별, 언어, 종교, 정치적 또는 기타 견해, 국가나 사회적 출신, 빈부, 출생 또는 장애인 자신이나 그 가족이 처하여 있는 상황에 따라 어떠한 종류의 구별이나 차별 없이 주어져야 한다.

3. 장애인은 인간으로서 존엄성을 존중받을 타고난 권리를 가진다. 장애인은 그 장애의 원인, 특질, 심각성에 관계없이 같은 연령의 일반 시민들과 동등하게, 가능한 정상적이고 풍족한 삶을 향유할 권리를 우선적으로 포함하는 기본권을 가진다.

4. 장애인은 타인과 동등한 시민권과 정치적 권리를 가진다. 「정신지체인 권리선언」 제7조는 정신지체인의 이와 같은 모든 권리의 어떠한 제한 또는 배제에도 적용된다.

5. 장애인은 가능한 한 자립하도록 하기 위하여 만들어진 시책을 활용할 자격을 가진다.

6. 장애인은 의학적·심리학적·기능적 치료 또는 의학적·사회적 재활, 교육, 직업 훈련, 재활, 원조, 고정 상담, 직업 알선 및 기타 장애인의 능력과 기능을 최대한 개발하여 사회를 통합 또는 재통합하는 과정을 촉진하는 서비스를 받을 권리가 있다.

7. 장애인은 경제적·사회적 보장을 받아 양질의 삶을 누릴 권리가 있다. 장애인은 그들의 능력에 따라 직업을 보장받고 고용되어 생산적이며 보수를 받는 직업에 종사하고 노동단체에 참여할 권리가 있다.

8. 장애인은 경제적·사회적 계획의 모든 단계에서 그 특별한 필요가 고려되는 자격을 갖는다.

9. 장애인은 가족이나 양부모와 함께 생활하고 모든 사회적·창의적 활동 및 여가 활동에 참여할 권리를 가진다. 장애인은 장애인의 거주가 문제시되지 않는다면, 그들이 요구한 조건과 다르게 취급받거나 그들이 유도한 발전에서 제외되어서는 아니 된다. 만약 장애인이 어느 특정 기관에 입소하여야만 한다면 그곳의 환경과 생활 조건은 가능한 한 같은 연령대의 일반인의 생활과 유사하여야 한다.

10. 장애인은 차별적·모욕적이거나 비열한 성질을 가진 모든 착취와 규제, 처우에서 보호받아야 한다.

11. 장애인은 자신의 인격과 재산을 보호하는 데 필수 불가결하게 도움이 필요할 경우에는 적절한 법적 도움을 받을 수 있어야 한다. 만약 장애인에 대하여 소송이 있을 경우, 그것에 적용되는 법적 수속에는 그들의 신체적·정신적 상태가 충분히 고려되어야 한다.

12. 장애인 단체는 장애인의 권리에 관한 모든 사항에 대하여 유효하게 협의할 수 있다.

13. 장애인과 가족 및 지역사회는 모든 적절한 수단을 통하여 이 선언에 포함된 권리를 충분히 고지받아야 한다.

정신지체인 권리선언

Declaration on the Rights of Mentally Retarded Persons

1971년 12월 20일, 총회 결의문 2856(XXⅥ)에 의하여 선언됨

총회는,

유엔 회원국들이 유엔 헌장에 의거하여 더 높은 생활수준과 완전고용, 경제적·사회적 진보 및 발전을 촉진시키기 위하여 유엔 기구와 상호 협력하여 공동의 또는 개별적 조치를 취하겠다는 협약에 유념하며,

인간의 권리 및 근본적 자유와 평화의 원리에 입각하여 유엔 헌장에서 표명하였던 인간의 존엄과 가치, 사회정의의 신념을 재확인하며,

「세계인권선언」, 「국제인권규약」, 「아동의 권리선언」, 「정신지체인 권리선언」의 여러 원칙들과 국제노동기구(ILO), 국제연합교육과학문화기구(UNESCO), 세계보건기구(WHO), 국제연합아동기금(UN Children's Fund) 및 기타 관련 기구의 규약, 협약, 권고 및 결의에서 사회 진보를 목적으로 이미 설정되었던 기준을 상기하며,

「사회 진보와 발전에 관한 선언」이 심신장애인의 권리 보호와 재활 및 복지 확보의 필요성을 제창하였던 사실을 강조하며,

정신지체인들이 다양한 활동 분야에서 자신의 능력을 발휘할 수 있도록 지원하고, 가능한 한 그들이 정상적인 생활로 통합될 수 있도록 촉진할 필요성이 있음을 유의하며,

일부 국가는 현재의 발전 단계에서 이러한 목적을 위하여 매우 제한된 노력밖에 기울일 수 없다는 사실을 인식하며,

본 「정신지체인 권리선언」을 선언하며, 다음과 같은 권리를 보호하기 위하여 공통적 기반과 준거 틀로 사용될 수 있도록 국내 및 국제적 행동을 촉구한다.

제1조 정신지체인은 최대한 실현 가능한 정도까지 다른 시민과 동등한 권리를 가진다.

제2조 정신지체인은 적절한 의료 혜택 및 신체 치료를 받을 권리를 가지며 그가 가진 능력과 가능성을 최대한 발전시킬 수 있도록 교육, 훈련, 재활, 지도를 받을 권리를 가진다.

제3조 정신지체인은 경제적 보호와 적절한 삶의 수준을 누릴 권리를 가진다. 정신지체인은 자신의 능력을 최대한 계발하기 위하여 생산적인 일을 수행하거나 기타 의미 있는 직업에 종사할 권리를 가진다.

제4조 가능한 언제든지 정신지체인은 그의 가족 또는 위탁 부모와 함께 살아야 하며 기타 다양한 형태로 지역사회 생활에 참여하여야 한다. 정신지체인과 함께 사는 가족은 지원을 받아야 한다. 만약 시설 보호가 필요하다면 정상인의 삶과 가능한 한 가장 유사한 환경과 조건이 조성되어야 한다.

제5조 정신지체인은 자신의 개인적 복지와 이익을 보호하기 위하여 필요할 경우 자격 있는 후견인을 둘 권리가 있다.

제6조 정신지체인은 착취, 학대 및 비인간적인 처우로부터 보호받을 권리가 있다. 만약 범죄행위로 인하여 기소된다면 그의 정신적 책임을 충분히 감안한 상태에서 공정한 재판을 받을 권리를 가진다.

제7조 정신지체인이 중증 장애로 인하여 그 모든 권리를 유용하게 행사할 수 없을 경우, 또는 그 권리의 일부나 전부가 제한되거나 배제되어야 할 필요가 생겼을 경우에 이를 적용하는 절차가 남용되지 않도록 적절한 법적인 보장을 받아야 한다. 이러한 절차는 자격을 갖춘 전문가에 의한 정신지체인의 사회적 행위능력 평가에 기초하여야 하며 정기적인 심사와 상급 기관에의 항소권을 전제하여야 한다.

카라카스 선언

Declaration of Caracas

PAHO/WHO 미국 지사의 후원으로 카라카스에서 1990년 11월 11일~14일 개최된 정신 의료 개편에 관한 라틴 아메리카 지역 회의에서, 1990년 11월 14일 만장일치로 채택됨

국회의원, 각종 협회, 보건 당국, 정신보건 전문가, 법학자가 지역보건 체계모델(Local health System Model)에서의 정신 의료 개편에 관한 라틴 아메리카 지역 회의에 모여 다음 사항에 주목하였다.

1. 기존의 전통적인 정신의학 서비스로는 지방분권적·참여적·통합적· 지속적인 예방 중심의 지역사회 기반 의료가 추구하는 목표들을 달성 할 수 없다.

2. 정신병원이 환자에게 제공되는 정신과 의료의 유일한 형태일 때, 전 술한 목적의 성취를 다음과 같이 방해한다.
    (a) 환자가 자신의 일상 환경으로부터 고립되어 결국 더 심각한 사 회적 장애를 일으킨다.
    (b) 환자의 인권과 시민권을 위태롭게 하는 불리한 환경을 창출한다.
    (c) 정신보건 의료를 위하여 국가에 할당된 재정 및 인적 자원의 대부분을 빼앗는다.
    (d) 국민의 정신보건 필요와 일반적인 보건 서비스 및 기타 분야에 적절한 전문적 교육 제공이 이루어지지 못한다.

또한 다음과 같은 내용을 고려하였다.

1. 1차 보건의료는 '2000년까지 만인에게 건강을'이라는 목표를 달성하는 수단으로서 WHO 및 PAHO에 의하여 채택되고 모든 회원국이 승인한 전략이다.

2. 지역보건체계모델은 지역 주민들의 보건 필요에 근거한 프로그램 개발을 위하여 더 나은 수준의 공급을 달성하는 수단으로서 이 지역 국가들에 의하여 수행되었고 지방분권화, 사회적 참여, 예방적 접근을 강조한다.

3. 정신보건 및 정신의학 프로그램은 이러한 보건의료 전달의 전략 및 모델에 근거한 원리와 지침을 통합하여야 한다.

선언

1. 1차 보건의료를 기초로 한 지역보건체계모델 틀 안에서 진행하는 정신과 의료의 개편은 지역사회에 근거하고, 사회 및 보건 네트워크로 통합되는 대안 서비스 모델을 촉진하게 할 것이다.

2. 지역에서 정신과 의료의 개편은 정신보건 서비스 전달에서 정신병원이 담당하는 지배적이고 집중적인 역할에 대한 비판적 검토를 포함한다.

3. 이용 가능하도록 만들어지는 자원, 의료 및 치료는

(a) 인간의 존엄과 인권 및 시민권을 보호하여야 한다.

(b) 합리적이고 기술적으로 적절한 기준에 근거하여야 한다.

(c) 환자가 자신의 지역사회에 머무를 것을 보장하도록 노력하여야
한다.

4. 필요하다면 다음의 사항에 대한 법률이 재입안되어야 한다.

(a) 정신장애인의 인권과 시민권은 보호되어야 한다.

(b) 정신보건 서비스 조직은 이러한 권리가 시행되도록 보장하여야
한다.

5. 정신보건 및 정신의학에 관한 교육은 개편 운동의 기초가 되는 원칙
에 따라 지역사회 보건 센터에 근거한 서비스 모델을 활용하여야 하
고 종합병원에서의 정신과 입원을 장려하여야 한다.

6. 이 회의의 조직, 협회, 기타 참가자들은 국가 수준에서 바람직한 개편
을 진척시킬 프로그램을 개발하고 옹호하는 책임을 맡아야 하며 동시
에 국내법 및 국제 협정에 따라 정신장애인의 인권을 지지하고 모니
터링하여야 한다.

이를 위하여 보건 및 법무부, 국회, 사회보장 및 기타 의료 제공 협회,
전문가 조직, 소비자 단체, 대학, 기타 교육기관, 정신과 의료 개편을
지지하는 미디어 등에 도움을 청하여 그 지역 주민에게 이익이 되는
성공적 발전을 보장하여야 한다.

하와이 선언/II

Declaration of Hawaii/II

1992년 세계정신의학협회(WPA) 총회에서 승인됨

문명이 시작된 이래 윤리는 치료술의 중요한 부분이다. 현대사회에서 의사와 환자 간의 헌신 및 기대의 충돌과 치료자와 환자 관계의 민감한 본질로 인하여 높은 윤리 기준은 의학적 특색으로서 정신의학 및 실행과 연관된 사람들에게 매우 중요하다는 것이 세계정신의학협회의 관점이다. 이 지침은 그러한 기준과의 밀접한 관계를 증진시키고 정신의학적 개념과 지식 및 기술의 남용을 예방하기 위하여 기술되었다.

정신과 의사는 의료 제공자일 뿐만 아니라 사회의 일원이므로 모든 의사에게 주어지는 윤리적 요구와 모든 사람에서의 사회적 책임과 더불어 정신 의학에 특별히 요구되는 윤리적 관계를 고려하여야 한다.

윤리적 행동은 정신과 의사 개인의 양심과 개인적 판단에 근거한다 하여도 전문직의 윤리적 관계를 명시화하기 위한 서면상의 지침이 필요하다.

따라서 세계정신의학협회 총회는 문화적 배경과 세계 다양한 나라에 존재하는 법적·사회적·경제적 수준에 큰 차이가 있음을 주지시키기 위하여 정신과 의사를 위한 다음의 윤리적 지침을 승인한다. 세계정신의학협회는 이 지침을 정신과 전문의의 윤리적 기준을 위한 최소한의 필요조건으로 간주한다.

1. 정신의학의 목표는 일반적으로 인정된 과학적 지식과 윤리적 원칙에 일관되게 최선의 능력을 발휘하여 정신장애를 치료하고 정신보건을 증진하는 것이며, 정신과 의사는 환자의 최선의 이익을 위하여 봉사하고 공익과 보건 자원의 적절한 할당에 관심을 가져야 한다. 이 목표를 달성하기 위하여 지속적인 연구와 보건의료 전문가, 환자, 그리고 공공의 지속적인 교육이 필요하다.

2. 모든 정신과 의사는 환자에게 그들의 지식을 동원하여 최선의 치료를 제공하여야 하며 환자가 받아들인다면 그들을 배려하여 치료하고 인간으로서의 고유한 존엄성을 존중하여야 한다. 정신과 의사는 다른 사람에 의하여 제공되는 치료에 대하여 책임이 있는 경우 충분한 감독과 교육을 제공할 의무를 가진다. 필요하거나 합당한 요청이 있을 경우 언제든지 정신과 의사는 다른 동료에게 도움을 요청하여야 한다.

3. 정신과 의사는 환자와 상호 동의에 기초한 치료 관계를 열망하여야 한다. 이의 최선을 위하여 신뢰, 비밀 보장, 협력 및 상호 책임이 요구된다. 몇몇 환자의 경우 이러한 관계 설정이 불가능할 수 있다. 그런 경우에는 환자의 친척이나 다른 가까운 사람과의 접촉이 이루어져야 한다. 법정신의학과 같이 치료 이외의 목적으로 관계가 이루어질 때는 관련된 사람에게 이러한 특성을 충분히 설명하여야 한다.

4. 정신과 의사는 환자에게 상태의 성격, 치료 절차, 가능한 대안, 예상되는 결과에 대하여 고지하여야 한다. 이러한 정보는 신중하게 전달되어야 하며 환자는 적합하고 가능한 치료 방법 중 선택할 기회를 가져야 한다.

5. 정신장애로 인하여 환자가 자신의 최고 이익을 판단할 수 없거나 그러한 치료 없이는 환자 자신 및 타인에게 심각한 손상을 줄 가능성이 있는 경우가 아니라면 환자 개인의 의도에 상반되는 어떠한 절차나 치료가 이루어질 수 없다.

6. 강제적 치료 조건이 더 이상 적용되지 않을 경우 정신과 의사는 환자에게 강제적 성격의 치료를 하지 않아야 하며, 그 이상의 치료가 이루어져야 할 경우에는 환자의 자발적 동의가 있어야 한다. 정신과 의사는 구금에 대하여 이의를 제기할 수 있는 장치와 환자의 안녕과 관련된 기타 사항에 대한 이의를 제기할 수 있다는 것을 환자나 친척, 기타 관계자에게 고지하여야 한다.

7. 정신과 의사는 절대로 개인이나 단체의 인권의 존엄성을 파괴하는 데 전문가적 가능성을 유용하여서는 아니 되며, 치료를 방해하는 부적절한 개인적 욕망, 감정, 선입견, 신념을 가져서는 아니 된다. 정신과 의사는 정신장애가 치료된 경우 자신의 직업을 어떤 도구로 활용하여서는 아니 된다. 만약 환자나 제3자가 과학적 지식이나 윤리적 원칙에 어긋나는 요구를 한다면 정신과 의사는 이를 거절하여야 한다.

8. 정신과 의사는 환자에게 듣거나 검사나 치료 중에 알게 된 내용이 무엇이든지 간에 환자가 이를 허락하거나 환자 자신 및 타인에게 발생할 수 있는 치명적인 피해를 예방하기 위한 것이 아니라면 반드시 비밀을 보장하여야 한다. 그러나 이 경우 환자에게 비밀 보호가 침해됨을 고지하여야 한다.

9. 정신의학 지식과 기술을 향상시키고 발전시키기 위하여서는 환자의 참여가 요구된다. 그러나 환자로부터 고지된 동의를 얻기 전까지 그 어떤 정보도 발표할 수 없으며, 동의를 얻어 개인 병력에 대하여 과학적 출판물을 발표할 때에도 환자의 인간 존엄성과 익명성을 지키고 대상자의 개인적 명예를 보호하기 위하여 합당한 모든 조치를 취하여야 한다. 환자의 참여는 자발적이어야 하며 연구 프로젝트의 목적, 과정, 위험 및 불편함에 대한 모든 정보와 예상되는 위험 및 불편함과 연구의 이익 간에 합당한 관계가 충분히 고지된 다음이어야 한다. 임상 연구에서 모든 연구 대상자는 환자로서의 고귀한 권리가 유지되고 지켜져야 한다. 아동이나 스스로 고지된 동의를 할 수 없는 환자의 경우 법률상 가까운 친척이 동의하여야 한다. 모든 환자나 연구 대상자는 이유가 무엇이든 어느 때든 자신이 참여한 교육, 연구 프로그램에서 참여를 중단할 수 있다. 프로그램 참여에 대한 거부는 물론이고 중단도 환자 또는 대상자를 돕는 정신과 의사의 노력에 영향을 주어서는 아니 된다.

10. 정신과 의사는 이 선언의 원칙에 어긋나는 모든 치료나 교육, 연구 프로그램을 중단하여야 한다.

정신의학과 인권에 대한 권고 1235

Recommendation 1235 on Psychiatry and Human Rights

유럽회의 의원 총회 – 1994 회기

1. 의회는 유럽회의의 회원국에 적용되는 정신의학에 관한 법률 및 시행에 관한 전반적인 연구가 없음을 확인하였다.

2. 한편으로 판례법 기구는 유럽인권위원회를 기초로 발전되어 왔고, 다른 한편으로 고문 방지와 비인간적 또는 수준 낮은 치료 또는 처벌 예방에 관한 유럽위원회는 정신의학의 배치 문제에 뒤따르는 실행과 관련된 수많은 의견을 제시하여 왔다는 것에 주목하였다.

3. 수많은 회원국에서 정신의학에 관한 법률이 검토되고 있거나 준비 중임에 주목하였다.

4. 많은 나라에서 정신과 치료 중 전두엽절제술, 전기충격요법, 성적 학대와 같은 특정 유형과 관련된 문제에 초점을 두고 활발하게 논쟁하고 있음을 안다.

5. 비자발적 환자로서 정신장애로 고통받는 환자의 법적 보호에 관하여 회원국을 향한 각료위원회의 권고 No. R(83)2를 상기한다.

6. 유럽회의 회원국은 정신장애인의 인권 존중을 보장하는 법적 조치를 채택하여야 할 때라고 생각한다.

7. 따라서 의회는 다음 규정에 근거한 새로운 권고문을 채택할 것을 각료 위원회에 요구하는 바이다.

(ⅰ) 입원 절차 및 조건

(a) 강제 입원은 예외적인 경우에만 행할 수 있으며, 다음의 기준을 따라야 한다.
- 환자나 타인에게 심각하게 위험한 경우
- 그대로 방치될 경우 환자 상태가 악화되거나 환자가 적절한 치료를 받지 못하게 된다면, 부가적인 기준이 환자 치료에 적용될 수 있다.

(b) 강제 입원의 경우 정신과 관련 시설로의 입원 결정은 심사자에 의하여 이루어져야 하고 그 시기는 구체적으로 지정되어야 한다. 입원 결정을 위한 준비는 반드시 정기적이고 자동적으로 심사되어야 한다. 향후 유럽회의의 생명윤리에 관한 협정에서 설정된 원칙은 모든 상황에서 존중되어야 한다.

(c) 결정 사항에 이의를 제기하는 데 대한 법적 규정이 마련되어야 한다.

(d) 정신과 관련 시설에 입원하는 즉시 환자의 권리에 관한 법 규약이 환자에게 제시되어야 한다.

(e) 1983년 비엔나에서 개최된 세계정신의학협회 총회에서 승인된 「하와이 선언」에 근거하여 무엇보다도 정신과 의사의 윤리에

관한 규약이 작성되어야 한다.

(ⅱ) 치료

(a) 신체장애인과 정신장애인이 구별되어야 한다.

(b) 환자나 환자 대리인이 지정한 개인, 변호인이나 후견인이 서면으로 된 고지된 승인을 하지 않고는, 또한 그러한 결정이 정신의학 전문가만으로 구성되지 않은 전문가 위원회에 의하여 확증되지 않고는 전두엽절제술과 전기충격요법이 시술되어서는 아니된다.

(c) 환자에게 제공되는 치료에 대하여 정확하고 상세한 기록이 남겨져야 한다.

(d) 정신장애인을 치료하기 위하여 적절한 훈련을 받았으며 충분한 자격을 갖춘 간호 인력이 있어야 한다.

(e) 환자는 치료 기관에 독립적인 '변호인'과 자유롭게 접촉할 수 있어야 한다. 마찬가지로 '후견인'은 미성년자의 이익을 도모할 책임이 있다.

(f) 고문 및 비인간적이거나 낮은 수준의 치료 또는 학대를 방지하기 위하여 유럽위원회 제도와 유사한 검열 제도가 마련되어야 한다.

(ⅲ) 정신의학에서의 문제점 및 학대

(a) 윤리 규약은 환자에 대한 의사의 성적 접촉 금지를 명확하게 규정하여야 한다.

(b) 격리 조치의 활용은 엄격하게 제한되어야 하며 대형 공동 시설
에서의 숙박 또한 피하여야 한다.

(c) 기계에 의한 강박은 이루어져서는 아니 된다. 약물 수단에 의한
강박은 추구하는 목적에 맞게 이루어져야 하며 개인의 출산할
권리에 대한 영구적 침해는 없어야 한다.

(d) 정신보건 분야에서의 과학적 연구는 환자의 이해 없이 환자 또
는 환자 대리인의 의지와 반대로 수행될 수 없으며 환자에게
유리한 범위 안에서만 수행되어야 한다.

(ⅳ) 구금된 사람의 경우

(a) 구금된 사람은 누구나 의사에게 진찰받아야 한다.

(b) 정신과 의사 및 특별히 훈련받은 직원이 각 형법 기관에 소속되
어야 한다.

(c) 앞서 기술된 규정과 윤리 규정은 구금된 사람에게 적용되어야
하며, 특히 이것이 구금의 필요와 양립할 수 있는 한 의학적 비밀
보장이 유지되어야 한다.

(d) 특정 형법 제도에는 성격장애로 고통받는 감금된 사람을 위한
사회 치료 프로그램이 설정되어 있어야 한다.

부록 2

'정신장애인의 인권 향상을 위한 지침' 및
인권 관련 국제 선언문의 영문본

Guidelines for the Promotion of Human Rights of Persons with Mental Disorders

Universal Declaration of Human Rights

Declaration on the Rights of Disabled Persons

Declaration on the Rights of Mentally Retarded Persons

Declaration of Caracas

Declaration of Hawaii/Ⅱ

Recommendation 1235(1994) on Psychiatry and Human Rights

GUIDELINES FOR THE PROMOTION OF HUMAN RIGHTS OF PERSONS WITH MENTAL DISORDERS

This document contains instruments for the assessment and the promotion of the respect of human rights of people with mental disorders, and the improvement of mental health care, according to major international documents on this issue, particularly a Resolution adopted by the UN General Assembly in 1991.

KEY WORDS : human rights, mental disorders, persons with mental disorders, mental health legislation.

MENTAL DISORDERS CONTROL
DIVISION OF MENTAL HEALTH AND
PREVENTION OF SUBSTANCE ABUSE
WORLD HEALTH ORGANIZATION
GENEVA
1996

ON THE INITIATIVE

WHO's "Initiative of Support to People Disabled by Mental Illness" is part of WHO's work on the prevention and treatment of mental disorders. It is an attempt to speed up the dissemination of information to governments and professionals about good community services for those with chronic mental illness and about new developments in this field. The initiative aims to help in reducing the disabling effects of chronic mental illness and to highlight social and environmental barriers which hinder treatment and rehabilitation efforts and which add to the stigma of chronic mental illness. It also stimulates consumer empowerment and involvement with planning, delivery and evaluation of mental health services.

The following sites have officially joined the Initiative and have participated in its various activities:

- The Queensland Northern Penninsula and Mackay Region Mental Health Service(centred in Townsville, Australia)
- British Columbia Ministry of Health — Mental Health Services(Vancouver, Canada)
- Centro Studi e Ricerche Salute Mentale — Regione Autonoma Friuli Venezia-Giulia, Trieste(Italy)
- Highland Health Board — Mental Health Unit and Highland Regional Council(Inverness, Scotland, UK)
- SOGG(Rotterdam) / Ministry of Health(The Netherlands)

The Dowakai Chiba Hospital(Funabashi, Japan) also takes part in some of the Initiative activities; other centres are at different levels of discussion concerning their joining the Initiative.

Further information on this Initiative can be requested to:

Dr J. M. Bertolote
Mental Disorders Control
WHO — Division of Mental Health and Prevention of Substance Abuse
1211 Geneva-27 Switzerland

INITIATIVE OF SUPPORT TO PEOPLE DISABLED BY MENTAL ILLNESS

CONSULTATIVE NETWORK

P. Alterwain, Uruguay

L. Bachrach, USA

P. Barham, UK

V. Basauri, Spain

J. Chamberlin, USA

P. Chanoit, France

F. Costa, Sweden

M. Farkas, USA

G. Harnois, Canada

T. Held, Germany

B. James, Australia

M. Jansen, USA

L. Lara Palma, Spain

G. Long, Canada

V. Nagaswami, India

D. Peck, UK

A. Pitta, Brazil

T. Powell, USA

H. Richards, UK

F. Rotelli, Italy

B. Saraceno, Italy

K. Schilder, The Netherlands

G. Scribner, Canada

T. Takizawa, Japan

H. Wagenborg, The Netherlands

R. Warner, USA

CONTENTS

ACKNOWLEDGEMENTS

Earlier drafts of these Guidelines benefited from the support and comments from many experts (listed below), whose opinions varied widely, as could be expected in view of the broad range of interests they represent. A brief discussion on their major point of divergence is found in the Introduction below. We are deeply grateful to them, as well as to the support provided by some of the non-governmental organizations they represent. The following, however, were instrumental in the production of these Guidelines: Dr E. M. Sommer, Mrs E. Fuller and Mr S. Poitras, Dr J. Orley and Dr S. Flache were always stimulating and provided insightful comments. Mrs T. Drouillet and Mrs N. Hurst went through the pains of typing and re-typing the several versions of this document.

J. E. Arboleda-Florez
WHO Collaborating Centre for Research
Calgary, Alb, Canada
Training in Mental Health
Calgary, Alb, Canada

P. Barham
Hamlet Trust
London, UK

A. Carmi
World Association for Medical Law
Haifa, Israel

J. Chamberlin
Center for Psychiatric Rehabilitation,
Boston University
Boston, MA, USA

P. S. Cohen
International Commission of Jurists
Chene-Bougeries, Switzerland

W. J. Curran*
WHO Collaborating Centre for Health
Legislation, Harvard School of Public
Health
Boston, MA, USA

G. Harnois
WHO Collaborating Centre for Research
and Training in Mental Health
Verdun, Que, Canada

E. Heim
International Federation of Psychotherapy
Bern, Switzerland

* Deceased

J. H. Henderson
Consultant in Mental Health
Weston Favell, Northampton, UK

A. Kraut
Buenos Aires, Argentina

C. Louzoun
European Committee on Law, Ethics and
Psychiatry
Paris, France

N. Macdermot
International Commission of Jurists
Chene-Bougeries, Switzerland

M. O'Hagan
World Federation of Psychiatric Users
Auckland, New Zealand

K. Pawlik
International Union of Psychological
Science
Hamburg, Germany

L. Eisenberg
Department of Social Medicine and Health
Policy, Harvard Medical School
Boston, MA, USA

G. Elvy
Canberra, Australia

C. Gendreau
Centre de Recherche en Droit Public
Universite de Montreal
Montreal, Canada

M. G. Giannichedda
Centro Franco Basaglia
Rome, Italy

L. O. Gostin
Georgetown/Johns Hopkins Program on
Law and Public Health
Washington, D.C., USA

T. Harding
Institut Universitaire de Médecine Légale
Geneva, Switzerland

N. Sartorius
World Psychiatric Association
Geneva, Switzerland

H. Sell
Regional Advisor for Health & Behaviour,
WHO Regional Office for South East Asia
New Delhi, India

E. Sorel
World Association for Social Psychiatry
Washington, D.C., USA

A. Szokoloczy-Grobet
Association Psychiatrie, Responsabilite et
Societe / Les Sans Voix
Geneva, Switzerland

J. G. V. Taborda
WHO Collaborating Centre for Research
and Training in Mental Health
Porto Alegre, Brazil

F. Torres Gonzalez
Mental Health Area, Granada University
Hospital
Granada, Spain

W. van den Graaf
Clientunion
Amsterdam, The Netherlands

INTRODUCTION

International instruments supporting even the most basic rights of persons with mental disorders have been very long in coming. On 17 December, 1991, the UN General Assembly adopted 25 Principles for the Protection of Persons with Mental Illness and the Improvement of Mental Health Care, through Resolution 46/119. This was the culmination of fourteen years of work that began in 1978 when the Human Rights Commission of the United Nations requested the Sub-commission on Prevention of Discrimination and Protection of Minorities to study the question of the protection of those detained on the basis of mental illness. The draft resolution was finalized after more than a decade of debates and discussions at the Economic and Social Council.

Its final format — as Principles — and its length: 25 Principles, some of which are very detailed — made it slightly different from previous UN resolutions related to other diseases or disabilities. The issue of course, was how to breathe life into this Resolution. Otherwise, the human right's interests in this worthwhile document were unlikely to be applied where they matter — in emergency rooms, hospital wards, outpatient treatment centres, courts and prisons. An additional tool which would facilitate its understanding and implementation was needed and there was general agreement that WHO should be in charge of the production of this tool. After consultations with experts and NGOs, a decision was made to produce guidelines, in the form of user-friendly questions to shed additional light on the Principles.

The Division of Mental Health and Prevention of Substance Abuse of the

World Health Organization has produced the Guidelines appearing hereafter, by which Resolution 46/119 may be operationalize by its signatories. The Guidelines were drafted for an in-depth assessment of the conditions related to each one of the major Principles in Resolution 46/119, as well as on its several sub-headings. In addition to traditional civil and political rights, the right to sound mental health treatment is embodied in Resolution 46/119. As such, the Guidelines also address basic quality assurance issues in order to provide a baseline from which policy-makers and mental health care providers may evaluate mental health programmes at the local, regional and national level.

In order to provide for a very brief general assessment of the human rights conditions of the mentally disordered at the country, regional or local level, a succinct Checklist derived from the Guidelines was also produced. Its main purpose is to allow for a quick assessment of the situation, as a companion tool to the more in-depth Guidelines.

Therefore, the present document is composed of three major parts: I. the Guidelines, in its full version; II. the Checklist; and III. the Appendices, including (i) the list of collaborators involved in the production of this document and (ii) some selected UN Declarations and Resolutions relevant to the mental health field in general.

In the text in Part I: Guidelines, we opted to include the highlighted text of the UN Resolution Principles, immediately followed by a series of relevant questions intended to guide those interested in verifying the extent to which each Principle is applied. It is not a scale with precise, definite or right/wrong answers; it is a qualitative instrument intended mostly to provide alternative approaches to the monitoring of each principle, making room for local characteristics, traditions and resources.

These questions are meant to illustrate what are some of the practical factors of the Principles. They do not aim to be exhaustive. Rather, they purport to raise examples of items for consideration and review. It is essential to note that not all questions may apply or be relevant everywhere, depending on a variety of factors such as culture, development level, legal tradition, political and religious systems and others.

However, the mere existence of the resolution and of guidelines for its implementation does not necessarily guarantee that people will benefit from them. In most cases it will be necessary that some official body (e.g. the Parliament, the Ministry of Health or Welfare, the Medical Council) ratify the Principles, or formally adopt them at national level. Next comes the verification of its enforcement, a task which some NGOs concerned with mental health and human rights issues are in an excellent position to perform.

Mental health legislation — and its enforcement — is profoundly important to development. According to the World Development Report published by the World Bank in 1993, the economic and public health burden of mental illness, measured in terms of DALYs(Disability-adjusted life years), the cost of mental disorders and related conditions (such as intentionally self-inflicted death of injury) is greatly deleterious to the process of social development.

Furthermore, adherence to the Rule of Law is important for social development in that it provides a predictable and codified set of norms and institutions which may be relied upon. As such, adherence to the Rule of Law is a stabilizing force in society. Mental health legislation — precisely because it is aimed at a vulnerable population subgroup — is an important first step in establishing or reinforcing the Rule of Law and thereby fostering social development.

Many people were approached during the process for the preparation of this document. It must also be said that some experts who were contacted expressed their dissatisfaction with the final text of the UN Resolution and hence with the ensuing Guidelines for its implementation and monitoring. The standpoint of these experts, who, generally speaking, represent users' (i.e. people with mental disorders) interests, reflects the decades old debate about the importance given to civil and political rights as opposed to the States' rights to issue coercive norms regarding health policy. In their viewpoint, the UN Resolution should have concentrated on "people's basic human rights" and not on "treatment rights", still in their view, the inclusion of treatment issues earlier during debates in the Sub-commission on Prevention of Discrimination and Protection of Minorities (particularly the modifications from the Daes Report to the subsequent Palley Report, which were maintained in the Steel Report) distorted its original intention, widened its scope and diluted the interest users had in it. Without taking issue on this question, it must be considered, nevertheless, that the UN Resolution represents a major international step forward both in terms of civil and political rights and of social, economic and cultural rights, and as such deserves to be given the appropriate means to be adequately disseminated and promoted, bearing in mind Chamberlin's words that:

"Perhaps someday it will be recognized that persons who have been diagnosed as mentally ill should have exactly the same rights as other citizens of their countries, most fundamentally the rights to live their lives as they choose and make their own decisions. Any special help or protection they may need as a result of disability should in no way alter their fundamental citizenship rights."

This document can only be useful if the above-mentioned conditions are satisfied and if it is widely available in local languages. Therefore, interested parties are encouraged to translate — and possibly adapt — it into local languages. The Division of Mental Health and Prevention of Substance Abuse would be grateful for copies of local editions, which should be forwarded to:

Dr J. M. Bertolote

Mental Disorders Control

Division of Mental Health and Prevention of Substance Abuse

World Health Organization

1211 Geneva-27 Switzerland

Part I

for the Application of the Principles for the Protection of Persons
with Mental Illness and the Improvement of Mental Health Care

Principles for the Protection of Persons with Mental Illness and the Improvement of Mental Health Care

The present Principles shall be applied without discrimination on any grounds, such as disability, race, colour, sex, language, religion, political or other opinion, national, ethnic or social origin, legal or social status, age, property or birth.

DEFINITIONS

In the present Principles:

(a) "Counsel"; means a legal or other qualified representative;

(b) "Independent authority" means a competent and independent authority prescribed by domestic law;

(c) "Mental health care" includes analysis and diagnosis of a person's mental condition, and treatment, care and rehabilitation for a mental illness or suspected mental illness;

(d) "Mental health facility" means any establishment, or any unit of an establishment, which as its primary function provides mental health care;

(e) "Mental health practitioner" means a medical doctor, clinical psychological, nurse, social worker or other appropriately trained and qualified person with specific skills relevant to mental health care;

(f) "Patient" means a person receiving mental health care and includes all persons who are admitted to a mental health facility;

(g) "Personal representative" means a person charged by law with the duty of representing a patient's interests in any specified respect or of exercising specified rights on the patient's behalf, and includes the parent or legal guarding of a minor unless otherwise provided by domestic law;

(h) "The review body" means the body established in acordance with principle 17 to review the involuntary admission of a patient in a mental health facility.

1. Are definitions of the above expressions (or equivalent concepts) under the body of law in force in keeping with the above definitions?

2. If variations exist between the above definitions and those under the body of law in force, is the body of law:

   a. more or less protective of patients' rights than the Principles?

   b. more or less aimed at the improvement of mental health care than the Principles?

GENERAL LIMITATION CLAUSE

The exercise of the rights set forth in the present Principles may be subject only to such limitations as are prescribed by law and are necessary to protect the health or safety of the persons concerned or of others, or otherwise to protect public safety, order, health or morals or the fundamental rights and freedom of others.

1. Is the exercise of any of the rights set forth in the Principles subject to limitations and, if so, which Principle and to what extent?

2. Is the exercise of the rights set forth in the Principles only subject to limitations prescribed by law? If not, how are those limitations prescribed? Are they set in advance? Are they known to the public?

3. Is the exercise of the rights set forth in the Principles only subject to limitations as are necessary to protect the health and safety of the person concerned or of others?

4. Is the exercise of he rights set forth in the Principles only subject to limitations as are necessary to protect public safety, order, health or morals or the fundamental rights and freedom of others?

5. Which are the specific grounds, if any are known, to limit the rights set forth in the present Principles in order:

a. to protect the health and safety of the persons concerned?

b. to protect the health and safety of others?

c. to protect public safety?

d. to protect public order?

e. to protect public health?

f. to protect public morals?

g. to protect the fundamental rights and freedom of others?

FUNDAMENTAL FREEDOMS AND BASIC RIGHTS

1. All persons have the right to the best available mental health care, which shall be part of the health and social care system.

1.1. Do all persons have the right to the best available mental health care? What mental health care is available, and to whom? Is the entire country in question divided into catchment areas such that geographically, all regions are within a catchment area? Are the catchment areas funded proportionately?

1.2. What importance is attributed to mental health care within the health care system? How are mental health services financed, as opposed to general health services, as evidenced by funding, reimbursement by third party payers, limitations on treatment which is reimbursed for mental health problems?

1.3. How are mental health, social, and general health services linked or integrated? Are they located near one another? If so, how near? If not, is transportation provided? Are they linked by a telecommunication system? If not, are couriers available?

1.4. Are there social services departments in mental health treatment facilities? If not, is there some entity whose task it is to act as liaison with collaborating mental health, general health and other facilities?

1.5. What social services are aimed at providing support for persons with a mental disorder? (Before, during and after treatment)

1.6. What is the difference between various population groups or geographical areas regarding:

- access to mental health care, for instance, how long is the average travel time to a mental health treatment facility in rural and urban areas?
- staff/patient ratios in mental health treatment facilities?

1.7. Within a given geographic area, what are the staff/patient ratios in mental health treatment facilities as opposed to staff/patient ratios in other types of health treatment facilities?

1.8. What neuropsychiatric drugs are available within a one hour walk? (See Principle 10, below.)

2. All persons with a mental illness, or who are being treated as such persons, shall be treated with humanity and respect for the inherent dignity of the human person.

2.1. Are all persons with a mental disorder treated with humanity and respect for their dignity?

2.2. Are there laws to guarantee this?

2.3. Are there ethical guidelines adopted by the professional societies of the various disciplines providing mental health care? What are the consequences of failure to respect these ethical guidelines?

2.4. Are all persons with a mental disorder informed of their rights on a timely basis in a format or language which they can understand?

3. All persons with a mental illness, or who are being treated as such persons, have the right to protection from economic, sexual and other forms of exploitation, physical or other abuse and degrading treatment.

3.1. Are persons with a mental disorder physically, sexually, economically or otherwise exploited? Conversely, how are they protected from such abuse? 3.2. Are there laws prohibiting such exploitation and abuse? Are there civil, criminal and/or administrative penalties for this type of exploitation and/or abuse? Are the criminal penalties greater for such exploitation, i.e. are mentally ill persons a "protected class", as is generally the case for minors? 3.3. Are there publicly available records of those who have been convicted of crimes involving the exploitation or abuse of members of a protected class, such that potential future employers have access to this information? (See also Principle 22.)

4. There shall be no discrimination on the grounds of mental illness. "Discrimination" means any distinction, exclusion or preference that has the effect of nullifying or impairing equal enjoyment, of persons with mental illness shall not be deemed to be discriminatory. Discrimination does not include any distinction, exclusion, or preference, undertaken in accordance with the provisions of the present Principles and necessary to protect the human rights of a person with a mental illness or of other individuals.

4.1. Is there evidence of discrimination (for example, in employment, in access to public services and amenities, in the criminal justice system) against persons with a mental disorder?

4.2. Are there laws prohibiting such discrimination? If so, are they enforced?

4.3. Are there any restrictions, in law or in practice, on the rights of persons with a mental disorder that do not exist for other members of the society, for example, freedom from unwanted treatment, or any of the privacy rights discussed under Principle 1(5) below?

4.4. What are the methods by which such a determination can be made? For example:

   a. Is there forced labour?

   b. Is comparable labour remunerated at the same rate when performed by those who are not mentally ill?

   c. What is the form of remuneration, i.e. is the patient ever paid with privileges, tokens for privileges or items, available for redemption only within the confines of the treating facility, or even freedom from punishment? In short, is the patient coerced into performing free or underpaid labour?

   d. Assuming the patient is paid, is this pavement made directly to the patient in the local currency? Is it paid to someone else, even for safekeeping?

4.5. Are there affirmative action programs for those with mental disorders?

5. Every person with a mental illness shall have the right to exercise all civil, political, economic, social and cultural rights as recognized

in the Universal Declaration of Human Rights, the International Covenant on Economic, Social and Cultural Rights, the International Covenant on Civil and Political Rights and in other relevant instruments, such as the Declaration on the Rights of Disabled Persons and the Body of Principles for the Protection of All Persons under Any Form of Detention or Imprisonments.

5.1. Are persons with a mental disorder able to exercise civil, political, economic, social and cultural rights, such as:

a. the right to marry?

b. the right to own property?

c. the right to freedom of thought, conscience and religion?

d. the right to vote?

e. the right to freedom of opinion and expression?

f. the right to work, to free choice of employment, to just and favourable conditions of work and to protection against unemployment?

g. the right to an education? (See also Principle 2, Protection of Minors.)

h. the right to have children and to maintain parental rights?

i. the right to freedom of movement and choice of residence (assuming the individual has not been involuntarily committed)?

j. the right to "qualified legal assistance to protect their rights, and to have their condition taken fully into account in any legal proceedings."[1]

---

1) See UN, "Declaration on the Rights of Disabled Persons"(1975), Principle 11 in Appendix.

k. the right to access to one's own medical records? (See also Principle 19, below.)

l. the right to freedom from cruel, inhuman or degrading treatment or punishment? (See generally, the *Declaration of the Rights of Disabled Persons*, in Appendix.)

6. Any Decision that, by reason of his or her mental illness, a person lacks legal capacity, and any decision that, in consequence of such incapacity, a personal representative shall be appointed, shall be made only after a fair hearing by an independent and impartial tribunal established by domestic law. The person whose capacity is at issue shall be entitled to be represented by a counsel. If the person whose capacity is at issue does not himself or herself secure such representation, it shall be made available without payment by that person to the extent that he or she does not have sufficient means to pay for it. The counsel shall not in the same proceedings represent a mental health facility or its personnel and shall not also represent a member of the family of the person whose capacity is at issue unless the tribunal is satisfied that there is no conflict of interest. Decisions regarding capacity and the need for a personal representative shall be reviewed at reasonable intervals prescribed by domestic law. The person whose capacity is at issue, his or her personal representative, if any, and any other interested person shall have the right to appeal to a higher court against any such decision.

6.1. What is the concept of capacity, or the lack thereof, within the country's legal system?

6.2. How is the concept limited?

   a. Incapacity to do what?

      i . stand trial?

      ii. write a will?

      iii. enter contracts?

      iv. make treatment decisions, including consent to release of information, experimental treatment or clinical trials?

   b. For how long?

      i . Is there any provision or procedure for restoration to capacity?

      ii. Is the matter reviewed automatically? If so, how often? Conversely, is the matter reviewed only upon request? If so, upon whose request?

6.3. What is the procedure for the determination of a person's legal capacity?

6.4. What are the consequences arising out of the decision that a person lacks legal capacity?

6.5. Is the person represented at the capacity hearing? By whom is any such person represented?

6.6. What measures are taken in case the person lacks sufficient means to pay for representation?

6.7. May the patient's counsel also represent any other interested party? For example, a mental health treatment facility (or its personnel) in the same proceedings, or a member of the person's family?

6.8. Who makes determinations as to conflict of interest? Do they apply a standard in making this determination? If so, what standard is applied?

6.9. Does the person have the right to an appeal? If so, what is the appeal procedure? Is the appeal made to the same body or to a higher authority? Are appeals accepted on the basis of substantive or procedural problems, or both?

6.10. Does anyone else have the right to appeal? If so, then who else has the right to do so? (Other possibilities might include treatment facilities, relatives, heirs, representatives or guardians, or those acting on behalf of minor children of the person in question.)

7. Where a court or other competent tribunal finds that a person with mental illness is unable to manage his or her own affairs, measures shall be taken, so far as is necessary and appropriate to that person's condition, to ensure the protection of his of her interests.

7.1. If a person is considered unable to manage his or her own affairs, what measures are taken to protect his or her interests? For example, the appointment of a guardian, a personal representative or a trustee?

7.2. What are the fiduciary duties of this representative? What, if any, are the consequences of failure to fulfil any such fiduciary duty? Are there administrative, civil and/or criminal penalties in the event of the abuse or exploitation of the incapacitated person?

PROTECTION OF MINORS

Special care should be given within the purposes of the principles and within the context of domestic law relating to the protection of minors to protect the rights of minors, including, if necessary, the appointment of a personal representative other than a family member.

1. What, if any, are the special measures taken to ensure the protection of minors with mental disorder?

2. What are the diagnostic categories for children?

3. Are those mental health professionals who treat minors with mental disorders specifically trained to work with children?

4. Do minor children have additional rights to confidentiality, for example, are juvenile court records sealed until the minor attains majority?

5. At what age are minors deemed to be able to give informed consent to treatment? At what age minors deemed to be able to give informed consent to release of information? Is this age different from the age at which a person is deemed to have reached majority for other purposes, for example,

voting, military service, jury duty, etc.?

6. Is the appointment of a personal representative other than a family member possible? If so, in what event? If not, then are there any special provisions for children in abusive of exploitative families? Who is generally appointed as a personal representative in the event of orphanage, abandonment, or court ordered termination of parental custody?

7. What, if any, are the provisions for education for minors with mental disorders, both within mental health treatment facilities and in the community? Are these schools or programmes accredited in the same manner as are other schools in the community?

8. Is there any special provision for the minor children of the mentally ill? For example, how are they cared for during a parent's hospitalization or after the parent has been determined to lack the capacity to care for the child?

LIFE IN THE COMMUNITY

Every person with a mental illness shall have the right to live and work, to the extent possible, in the community.

1. Is every person with a mental disorder able to live and work outside the hospital, assuming that they are medically stable?

2. Specifically, are there living arrangements tailored to the needs of those with mental disorders? If so, do they exist in adequate quantity to fulfill the need within the community? Are these facilities public or private?

3. Are there possibilities for those with mental disorders to work outside the hospital? Are there vocational rehabilitation programs to foster independence?

4. Are these facilities and/or programmes within the financial reach of the population for which they were designed?

5. What is the average duration of an inpatient psychiatric hospitalization?
   a. In a given facility?
   b. In a given region?
   c. In the country as a whole?

6. Is there a specific budget set aside by one or more ministries to support reintegration efforts? How is it allocated?

7. What are the measures taken for psychosocial rehabilitation during and after hospitalization?

8. What social and health services are available within the community?

9. Are patients oriented to the available social and health services in their community prior to discharge?

10. What are the contacts with other treatment facilities, schools or social agencies?

11. What are the living and aftercare arrangements for patients after discharge from an inpatient mental health treatment facility? For example, are there halfway houses, supportive apartments, community mental health centres, partial hospital or day programs, crisis centres? Are those available as parts of a gradual plan of social reintegration?

12. Are these facilities sufficient to meet the needs within the community?

13. Are these facilities inspected by the health authorities? If so, which ones?

14. Are these facilities accredited and/or licensed in the same manner as are hospitals?

15. What are the consequences, if any, of failure to achieve any such accreditation or license?

16. Are there opportunities for private housing initiatives to be state-funded? For example, are there municipal bonds issued for the construction and maintenance of such housing facilities?

DETERMINATION OF MENTAL ILLNESS

1. A determination that a person has a mental illness shall be made in accordance with internationally accepted medical standards.

1.1. What are the standards for the determination of mental disorder? (ICD; DSM-IV, other?)

1.2. In what way is every patient evaluated?

   a. Who performs the evaluation?

   b. Where are the evaluations performed?

   c. Is there access to other assessment tools? For example, is there access to neurological testing? Is there access to psychological testing? Are there laboratory facilities equipped for urine and blood tests? Are medical records generally available, assuming the patient has given informed consent to their review?

2. A determination of mental illness shall never be made on the basis of political, economic or social status, or membership in a cultural, racial or religious group, or for any other reason not directly relevant to mental health status.

2.1. Does the political, economic or social status of the person have any bearing on a diagnosis of mental disorder?

2.2. Does membership in any cultural, racial or religious group have any bearing on a diagnosis of mental disorder?

2.3. Does any factor not directly relevant to the person's mental status have any bearing on a diagnosis of mental disorder?

2.4. Is non-conformity with prevailing moral, social, cultural or political values considered to be a determining factor in the diagnosis of a mental disorder?

3. Family or professional conflict, or non-conformity with moral, social, cultural or political values or religious beliefs prevailing in a person's community, shall never be a determining factor in the diagnosis of mental illness.

3.1. Are family or professional conflicts considered to be a determining factor in the diagnosis of mental disorder?

3.2. Are any other factors not directly relevant to the person's mental status considered to be a determining factor in the diagnosis of mental disorder?

4. A background of past treatment of hospitalization as a patient shall not of itself justify any present of future determination of mental illness.

Does past treatment or hospitalization for mental disorder in itself justify any present of future determination of mental disorder?

5. No person or authority shall classify a person as having, or otherwise indicate that a person has, a mental illness except for purpose directly relating to mental illness or the consequences of mental illness.

In summary, are people ever diagnosed as mentally ill for reasons other than mental status? Is there data available to establish the correlations listed above, if they should exist? For example, are there comparative studies of what groups have been hospitalized, under what conditions, for how long, which contain breakdowns of these factors, such as race, religion, language, political persuasion, etc?

MEDICAL EXAMINATION

No person shall be compelled to undergo medical examination with a view to determining whether or not he or she has a mental illness except in accordance with a procedure authorized by domestic law.

1. Is anyone compelled to undergo medical examination if legal provision governing this is absent?

2. Under domestic law, can a person be compelled to undergo a mental status examination(MSE)? If so, when? Examples might include an MSE being included as a part of emergency room procedure. Such an examination might also be made under court order to determine capacity, competency, parental fitness, parole status, etc.

3. Who performs such examinations?

4. Who pays for the performance of these examinations?

5. Is informed consent required prior to the MSE? Is informed consent obtained prior to the MSE?

6. Does the patient have the right and/or the opportunity to seek a second opinion?

CONFIDENTIALITY

The right of confidentiality of information concerning all persons to whom the present Principles apply shall be respected.

1. Do all those with legal access to the patient and/or his records fully respect the patient's right to confidentiality?

2. Who specifically has the duty of maintaining confidentiality? (Consider information divulged in self-help groups or outside the normal treatment setting. Consider also information divulged to non-clinical staff of the treating facility.)

3. How is confidentiality protected?

4. Are written consent forms presented in a language and format that the patient can fully understand and required to be signed by the patient or his legal representative prior to any release of information?

5. If so, are the consents general or limited?

6. If they are limited, in what way are they limited? For example, can the patient control to whom his confidential information will be conveyed? Can

the patient limit the subject matter of the information to be conveyed? Can the patient the information can be used?

7. What are the consequences and/or penalties for failure to respect and protect a patient's confidentiality?

8. Under what circumstances can confidentiality be breached?

9. Under what circumstances must confidentiality be breached? (Justifiable circumstances for such a breach might include life threatening emergencies, public safety, or under court order.)

ROLE OF COMMUNITY AND CULTURE

1. Every patient shall have the right to be treated and cared for, as far as possible, in the community in which he or she lives.

> 1.1. How far away (consider both distance and difficulty of standard journey) from his home is the patient being treated? Do comparable facilities exist closer to the patient's home?

2. Where treatment takes place in a mental health facility, a patient shall have the right, whenever possible, to be treated near his or her home of the home of his or her relatives or friends and shall have the right to return to the community as soon as possible.

> 2.1. How long after completed treatment does the patient return to the community?
>
> 2.2. How is the patient reintegrated into the community? (See Principle 3, above.)

3. Every patient shall have the right to treatment suited to his or her cultural background.

> 3.1. Is every patient treated taking into account his or her cultural

background?

3.2. How is this ensured?

3.3. What are the limitations on this principles? For example, if a patient were to refuse treatment on religious grounds, carried a diagnosis of schizophrenia, and when unmedicated, suffered from religious delusions, would the patient's religious beliefs be respected, or would the treating facility request that a guardian be appointed in order to gain legal consent for treatment?

STANDARDS OF CARE

1. Every patient shall have the right to receive such health and social care as is appropriate to his or her health needs, and is entitled to care and treatment in accordance with the same standards as other ill persons.

1.1. Are quality assurance standards being upheld? If so, what standards?[2]

1.2. Are there differences between the standards of social and health care for those who suffer from mental, as opposed to physical, disorders or illnesses?

1.3. Does every patient receive such health and social care as is appropriate to his/her health needs?

1.4. What are the standards of care compared to those for physically ill persons?

1.5. If patients are unable to care for their own hygiene, are they assisted in doing so?

1.6. As an outpatient, how long does it take for a person in need to be seen by a mental health practitioner?

1.7. What procedures are in place for emergency treatment?

1.8. Do psychiatric patients routinely receive a full medical examination on

---

2) Consider those set forth in WHO – Division of Mental Health, "Quality Assurance in Mental Health Care(Vol. 1)"(1994).

admission? If not, when do they receive one, if at all?

1.9. What is the frequency of medical examination thereafter for both chronic and acute patients?

1.10. Does every patient have some space which may be considered his/her own?

1.11. Are essential drugs for the treatment of mental disorders available? (See Principle 10, below.)

2. Every patient shall be protected from harm, including unjustified medication, abuse by other patients, staff or others or other acts causing mental distress or physical discomfort.

2.1. How is each patient protected from harm, including unjustified medication?

2.2. How are treatment modalities monitored? Are treatment decisions, particularly medication review, plans for restraint or isolation, discussed in multidisciplinary staff meetings?

2.3. Are treatment decisions reviewed on a regular basis? If so, at what intervals? If not, how are they made? Are all staff members trained in appropriate and least restrictive methods of restraint, as well as cardio-pulmonary resuscitation and basic first aid? (See §§2.11.~2.14., below.)

2.4. Which forms of restraint are allowed and which are not?

2.5. Are there written procedures for the use of isolation and restraint?

2.6. Are medication orders left such that nursing staff may administer drugs on an "as needed" basis? If so, is this practice ever abused for the convenience of staff?

2.7. Do all staff members routinely receive supervision from other staff members?

2.8. How is each patient protected from abuse by other patients or staff?

2.9. Are violent patients housed with non-violent patients?

2.10. What is the staff to patient ratio during the day shift? What is the staff to patient ratio during the night shift? Are these ratios adequate to cover the acuity of need on the unit or ward?

2.11. Is the unit overpopulated?

2.12. What are the provisions made for dangerous items or materials, "shapes"? Are they kept in a locked or inaccessible area?

2.13. Are patient's belongings searched upon admission and after off grounds passes?

2.14. Are patient's tested for communicable diseases prior to admission? In the case of the human immunodeficiency virus, is this considered violative of the patients human rights? Are universal precautions observed? Are safety measures taken against intimate contact between patients or between patients and staff?

TREATMENT

1. Every patient shall have the right to be treated in the least restrictive environment and with the least restrictive or intrusive treatment appropriate to the patient's health needs and the need to protect the physical safety of others.

> 1.1. Is each patient treated in the least restrictive environment which is medically necessary and with the least restrictive or intrusive form of treatment that is medically necessary? (See Principle 8, §§2.2.~2.3., above.)
>
> 1.2. How often is the need for restrictions re-evaluated?

2. The treatment and care of every patient shall be based on an individually prescribed plan, discussed with the patient, reviewed regularly, revised as necessary and provided by qualified professional staff.

> 2.1. Is there an individually prescribed plan for treatment and care?
>
> 2.2. Is it discussed with the patient? Does the patient sign the treatment plan?
>
> 2.3. Is the patient's care discussed with the family, after consent from the patient or personal representative? Upon request, or as a matter of course?
>
> 2.4. Is the patient kept informed about his own progress?

2.5. How often is the treatment plan reviewed? Is the treatment plan automatically reviewed periodically?

2.6. How often are staff meetings held to discuss the patient's care plan?

2.7. Is the treatment plan revised as necessary?

2.8. Who provides the treatment?

2.9. Is the treatment plan appropriate for the patient's culture, religion, clinical condition and age?

3. Mental health care shall always be provided in accordance with applicable standards of ethics for mental health practitioners, including internationally accepted standards such as the Principles of Medical Ethics relevant to the role of health personnel, particularly physicians, in the protection of prisoners and detainees against torture and other cruel, inhuman or degrading treatment or punishment, adopted by the United Nations General Assembly. Mental health knowledge and skills shall never be abused.

3.1. What are the standards of ethics to which mental health provides refer?

3.2. Is there evidence to suggest that mental health care providers have taken any part in torture or other cruel, inhuman or degrading treatment or punishment?

3.3. Are mental health care providers required, under local law, to report torture or other cruel, inhuman or degrading treatment of patients of which they are aware? To whom?

3.4. Is there any evidence which suggests that mentally ill patients are subjected to abuse more often than patients in general? What are the afeguards against such abuse? (See Principle 8, §2., above.)

3.5. What are the consequences of established violations of the standards of ethics in force?

4. The treatment of every patient shall be directed towards preserving and enhancing personal autonomy.

4.1. Does treatment of every patient preserve and enhance personal autonomy?

4.2. To that end, are the rights of the patient safeguarded?

4.3. Is individual empowerment a treatment priority? (See Principle 8, §1.9., above.)

4.4. Is outpatient care preferred over impatient care?

4.5. Is community-based care preferred over institutional care?

4.6. Do supportive living situations exist in the community so that those nominally able to live outside the hospital are provided with an opportunity to do so?

PRINCIPLE 10

MEDICATION

1. Medication shall meet the best health needs of the patient, shall be given to a patient only for therapeutic or diagnostic purposes and shall never be administered as a punishment or for the convenience of others. Subject to the provisions of paragraph 15 of principle 11 below, mental health practitioners shall only administer medication of known or demonstrated efficacy.

1.1. Are there any written guidelines on the indications and use of drug therapies?

1.2. Does use of drug therapy follow internationally accepted guidelines for mental health care?[3]

1.3. Is all medication employed of a known or demonstrated efficacy? Is it approved for use by local law? Is all medication approved for the specific purpose for which it being employed?

1.4. Is medication ever administered as a punishment or for the convenience of others?

1.5. How is it ensured that medication is administered for therapeutic and/or diagnostic purposes only?

---

3) Consider, for instance, WHO, "Essential Drugs in Psychiatry"(1994).

2. All medication shall be prescribed by a mental health practitioner authorized by law and shall be recorded in the patient's records.

2.1. Who is responsible for prescription and administration of medication?

2.2. Are staff members taking part in decisions regarding patient medication?

2.3. Is all medication recorded? By whom?

2.4. Where is all medication recorded?

2.5. Which medical drugs are included in the basic drug supply of the mental health facility?

2.6. Which psychiatric drugs are included in this basic drug supply?

2.7. Does the supply include the psychoactive essential drugs listed by WHO?[4]

2.8. Which neuropsychiatric drugs are available within one hour's walk?

2.9. Who prescribes them?

2.10. What is the nature of administration? Is medication administered in a clinic, a hospital, in the patient's home, group home or supportive apartment?

2.11. What quality assurance measures are taken to assure proper administration?

2.12. What follow up care is provided? For example, are periodic blood samples taken to determine lithium levels, are depressed patients monitored

---

4) Amitriptyline and/or imipramine, biperiden, carbamazapine, chlorpromazine and haloperidol, clomipramine, diazepam, fluphenazine, lithium carbonate, and phenobarbital. WHO, "The Use of Essential Drugs"(1995), WHO Technical Report Series No. 850.

routinely for suicidality, are those receiving antipsychotic medications routinely monitored for EPS?

2.13. Are routine medication inventories conducted in order to detect theft or unauthorized use? Are they performed by different people?

CONSENT TO TREATMENT

1. No treatment shall be given to a patient without his or her informed consent, except as provided for in paragraphs 6, 7, 8, 13 and 15 of the present principle.

1.1. Is the patient's informed consent requested prior to treatment?

1.2. Do patients give informed consent prior to treatment? If not, is the refusal to consent respected, or is treatment administered against the patient's will?

1.3. Is the patient requested to sign a consent form? Do patients generally sign consent forms?

1.4. Is the patient informed that the treatment cannot be legally administered without his or her consent?

1.5. Is the patient informed that the consent is revocable?

1.6. How is the consent obtained?

2. Informed consent is consent obtained freely, without threats or improper inducements, after appropriate disclosure to the patient of adequate and understandable information in a form and language understood by the patient on:

(a) The diagnostic assessment;

(b) The purpose, method, likely duration and expected benefit of the proposed treatment;

(c) Alternative modes of treatment, including those less intrusive;

(d) Possible pain of discomfort, risks and side-effects of the proposed treatment.

2.1. Are patients entitled to consent to treatment freely? Are threats or improper inducements made to patients to lead them to consent to treatment? (Examples include undue threat of reducing one's access to treatment, undue threat of altering one's living conditions and undue inducements by reference to the impact of declining treatment on third parties.)

2.2. Are patients informed of a diagnostic assessment?

2.3. Are patients informed of the purpose, method, likely duration and expected benefit of the proposed treatment?

2.4. Are patients informed of alternative modes of treatment?

2.5. Are patients informed of the possible pain or discomfort, risks and side effects of the proposed treatment?

2.6. In what form of language is this information conveyed?

2.7. Does all this information exist in writing in an appropriate language? If so, is this documentation given to the patient? Can the patient in question read? If not, is this document read to him or her?

2.8. What are the instruments put into place to foster adequate information for patients?

2.9. Is the patient competent to give informed consent? If not, then who is, and is that individual or body consulted in accordance with local law? [See Principle 1(6), above.]

3. A patient may request the presence of a person or persons of the patient's choosing during the procedure for granting consent.

3.1. Is the patient guaranteed the right and time to request the presence of a person or persons of his or her choosing during the procedure for granting consent?

3.2. Who may be present during the procedure for granting consent?

3.3. May the patient consult with the person or persons in private prior to granting such consent?

4. A patient has the right to refuse or stop treatment, except as provided for in paragraphs 6, 7, 8, 13 and 15 of the present principle. The consequences of refusing or stopping treatment must be explained to the patient.

4.1. Is the patient informed that he has the right to refuse or stop treatment?

4.2. Is the patient informed about the consequences of refusing or stopping treatment?

4.3. Are patients ever made to fear retribution for refusal of treatment?

4.4. Can treatment be compulsory? If so, when?

4.5. Is all involuntary treatment (and justification) documented in the patient's record?

5. A patient shall never be invited or induced to waive the right to informed consent. If the patient should seek to do so, it shall be explained to the patient that the treatment cannot be given without informed consent.

5.1. Are patients ever invited or induced to waive the right to informed consent?

5.2. What protections exist to prevent this practice?

6. Except as provided in paragraphs 7, 8, 12, 13, 14 and 15 of the present principle, a proposed plan of treatment may be given to a patient without a patient's informed consent if the following conditions are satisfied:

(a) The patient is, at the relevant time, held as an involuntary patient;

(b) An independent authority, having in its possession all relevant information, including the information specified in paragraph 2 of the present principle, is satisfied that, at the relevant time, the patient lacks the capacity to give or withhold informed consent to the proposed plan of treatment or, if domestic legislation so provides, that, having regard to the patient's own safety or the safety of others, the patient unreasonably withholds such consent;

(c) The independent authority is satisfied that the proposed plan of treatment is in the best interest of the patient's health needs.

6.1. Is treatment ever given without consent? If so when?

6.2. If there is treatment without consent, are the following three conditions satisfied?

a. Is the patient involuntary?

b. Is an independent authority satisfied that the patient lacks the capacity to give or withhold informed consent or that the patient unreasonably withholds such consent?

c. Is the independent authority satisfied that the proposed treatment is in the best interests of the patient's health needs?

6.3. In what percentage of all treated cases is mandatory treatment administered?

6.4. Are there studies or data available which demonstrate the long-term efficacy of involuntary as opposed to voluntary treatment?

6.5. What of the possibility of restoration to capacity? Is it likely? If so, could the contemplated treatment be delayed until such time as capacity is restored, without undue harm as a result of such delay? [See Principle 11(9), below.]

7. Paragraph 6 above does not apply to a patient with a personal representative empowered by law to consent to treatment for the patient; but, except as provided in paragraphs 12, 13, 14 and 15 of the present principle, treatment may be given to such a patient without his or her informed consent if the personal representative, having been given the information described in paragraph 2 of the present principle, consents on the patient's behalf.

7.1. Is the personal representative authorized to consent, on the patient's behalf, to:

    a. Sterilization?

    b. Medical or surgical procedures?

    c. Psychosurgery or other intrusive and irreversible treatments for mental disorder?

    d. Clinical trials and experimental treatment?

7.2. If the personal representative withholds consent, is this decision respected?

7.3. Is there an appeal process regarding the personal representative and/or his/her decisions? Who may make such an appeal? Possibilities include the patient, the treating facility, the clinician, the patient's family members, etc.

8. Except as provided in paragraphs 12, 13, 14 and 15 of the present principle, treatment may also be given to any patient without the patient's informed consent if a qualified mental health practitioner authorized by law determines that it is urgently necessary in order to prevent immediate or imminent harm to the patient or to other persons. Such treatment shall not be prolonged beyond the period that is strictly necessary for this purpose.

8.1. Who may determine the emergency status of a situation? How many signatures are required in order to involuntarily commit a person? Whose signatures are required?

8.2. What is considered to be an emergency situation? Is the concept of emergency or urgency limited to imminent danger of harm to self or others?

8.3. Does the category of emergency involuntary treatment specifically exclude:

　　a. Sterilization?

　　b. Psychosurgery or other intrusive and irreversible treatments for mental disorder?

　　c. Clinical trials and experimental treatment?

8.4. How long is such treatment extended?

8.5. Does involuntary commitment require a court order?

8.6. What are the time limits on involuntary commitment? Are these fixed by statute and reviewed periodically as a matter of course? Conversely, are time limits set by the court, the personal representative, or by the clinicians authorizing the involuntary commitment?

9. Where any treatment is authorized without the patient's informed consent, every effort shall nevertheless be made to inform the patient about the nature of the treatment and any possible alternatives and to involve the patient as far as practicable in the development of the treatment plan.

9.1. Having been given treatment without consent, is the patient nevertheless informed about the nature of the treatment, including any side effects, and any possible alternatives?

9.2. How has the patient been involved in the development of the treatment plan to the extent possible?

10. All treatment shall be immediately recorded in the patient's medical records, with an indication of whether involuntary or voluntary.

10.1. Is shall treatment recorded?

10.2. In what format?

10.3. Where?

10.4. When?

10.5. By whom?

10.6. Are there recognized standards of documentation, especially regarding medication?

11. Physical restraint or involuntary seclusion of a patient shall not be employed except in accordance with the officially approved procedures of the mental health facility and only when it is the only means available to prevent immediate or imminent harm to the patient or others. It shall not be prolonged beyond the period which is strictly necessary for this purpose. All instances of physical restraint or involuntary seclusion, the reasons for them and their nature and extent shall be recorded in the patient's medical record. A patient who is restrained or secluded shall be kept under humane conditions and be under the care and close and regular supervision of qualified members of the staff. A personal representative, if any and if relevant, shall be given prompt notice of any physical restraint or involuntary seclusion of the patient.

11.1. Under what circumstances is physical restraint or involuntary seclusion employed?

11.2. What are the specific objectives of the use of physical restraint or involuntary seclusion?

11.3. How long are patients restrained or secluded? Is the practice restricted to a necessary period?

11.4. Is every incident of physical restraint or involuntary seclusion documented? Does this documentation include the justification for, and he nature and extent of the restraint or seclusion? Where is this documentation placed?

11.5. Under what conditions is the restrained patient kept?

11.6. Who is informed about the patient's physical restraint or involuntary seclusion? After what period of time?

12. Sterilization shall never be carried out as a treatment for mental illness.

12.1. Is sterilization performed as a treatment for mental disorder? If so, under what circumstances?

12.2. How often has this happened recently (e.g. during the last 18 months)?

12.3. Does this occur more or less frequently than it has in the past?

12.4. Is sterilization performed as a treatment, of for other stated purposes, on any group disproportionately?

13. A major medical or surgical procedure may be carried out on

a person with mental illness only where it is permitted by domestic law, where it is considered that it would best serve the health needs of the patient and where the patient gives informed consent, except that, where the patient is unable to give informed consent, the procedure shall be authorized only after independent review.

13.1. In case a major medical or surgical procedure is carried out on a patient with a mental disorder, does the patient give his informed consent?

13.2. What is done if the patient is unable to do so?

13.3. What are the reasons for this procedure?

13.4. Is the procedure necessary immediately, or could it be delayed until the patient is restored to capacity to make this sort of decision independently without causing the patient undue harm? Who makes the determination?

14. Psychosurgery and other intrusive and irreversible treatments for mental illness shall never be carried out on a patient who is an involuntary patient in a mental health facility and, to the extent that domestic law permits them to be carried out, they may be carried out on any other patient only where the patient has given informed consent and an independent external body has satisfied itself that is genuine informed consent and that the treatment best serves the health needs of the patient.

14.1. When are psychosurgery and other intrusive and irreversible treatments generally performed?

14.2. Is it ensured that the patient is not an involuntary patient?

14.3. Who gives approval?

14.4. Can a guardian or personal representative's authority extend this far?

15. Clinical trials and experimental treatment shall never be carried out on any patient without informed consent, except that a patient who is unable to give informed consent may be admitted to a clinical trial or given experimental treatment, but only with the approval of a competent, independent review body specifically constituted for this purpose.

15.1. Are patients with mental disorders participants in clinical trials or experimental treatment? If so, when?

15.2. Is informed consent required? [See Principle 11(1).] Does the patient give informed consent?

15.3. If the patient is unable to do so, who gives approval?

15.4. Does a personal representative or guardian have the authority to consent to the patient's participation in clinical trials or experimental treatment?

16. In the cases specified in paragraphs 6, 7, 8, 13, 14 and 15 of the present principle, the patient or his or her personal representative, or any interested person, shall have the right to appeal to a judicial or other independent authority concerning any treatment given to him or her.

16.1. Are patients treated without informed consent? [See also Principle 11(1).]

16.2. Are psychosurgery and other irreversible or intrusive treatments carried out on patients?

16.3. If the answer to 16.1. and 16.2. is "yes", then: Who is given the right to appeal to an authority? In the event that the court determines that the actions taken were not warranted or were improperly authorized, what are the consequences of such a determination? For example, in the event that irreversible treatment has been carried out, does the patient or his family have an actionable claim in civil court against the treating facility and/or clinicians? Is such treatment considered illegal? If so, can criminal penalties be enforced against the facility and/or clinician in the event that the process was only invasive and not irreversible?

16.4. What is the appropriate authority for such an appeal?

NOTICE OF RIGHTS

1. A patient in a mental health facility shall be informed as soon as possible after admission, in a form and a language which the patient understands, of all his or her rights in accordance with the present Principles and under domestic law, and the information shall include an explanation of those rights and how to exercise them.

1.1. Is the patient in a mental health facility informed about all his/her rights?

1.2. When is the patient informed?

1.3. Is the patient provided with this information in a format and language he/she can understand?

1.4. Does the patient know how to exercise these rights?

1.5. Does a patient with the necessary capacity have the right to nominate a person who should be informed on his/her behalf?

1.6. Does the patient have the right to nominate a person to represent his/her interests with the authorities of the facility?

1.7. Is the patient free from punishment or legitimate fear of retribution with regard to the exercise of his or her rights?

1.8. In case the patient is unable to understand such information, who is informed on his/her behalf?

2. If and for so long as a patient is unable to understand such information, the rights of the patient shall be communicated to the personal representative, if any and if appropriate, and to the person or persons best able to represent the patient's interests and willing to do so.

2.1. Who is informed on the patient's behalf?

2.2. Who represents the patient with the authorities?

a. a friend?

b. a defined personal representative?

3. A patient who has the necessary capacity has the right to nominate a person who should be informed on his or her behalf, as well as a person to represent his or her interests to the authorities of the facility.

3.1. Who appoints this representative?

3.2. What are the substantive and temporal limitations on the authority of this personal representative? [See also Principle 1(7), above.]

RIGHTS AND CONDITIONS IN MENTAL HEALTH FACILITIES

1. Every patient in a mental health facility shall, in particular, have the right to full respect for his or her:

(a) Recognition everywhere as a person before the law;

(b) Privacy;

(c) Freedom of communication, which includes freedom to communicate with other persons in the facility; freedom to send and receive uncensored private communications; freedom to receive, in private, visits from a counsel or personal representative and, at all reasonable times, from other visitors; and freedom of access to postal and telephone services and to newspapers, radio and television;

(d) Freedom of religion or belief.

1.1. Are internationally-accepted guidelines for mental health care being followed?[5]

1.2. Is there full respect for recognition of the patient as a person before the law?

1.3. Is there full respect for the patient's privacy? For example:

---

5) Consider, for instance, WHO, "Essential Treatments in Psychiatry"(1994).

a. Can toilets and bathrooms be locked from the inside?

b. If body inspection or urine screens are necessary, is full respect for the person's privacy accorded?

1.4. Is there full respect for the sexual autonomy of the patient? Is sexual harassment or abuse of patients tolerated?

1.5. Is there full respect for the patient's freedom of communication, for instance:

a. Does the patient have the right to communicate with other persons in the facility?

b. Is the patient free to send and receive uncensored private communication?

c. Is the patient free to receive, in private, visits from counsel or a personal representative and from other visitors?

1.6. Is the patient free to express and practice his/her religion or belief?

1.7. Is the patient free to access newspapers, radio and television?

2. The environment and living conditions in mental health facilities shall be as close as possible to those of the normal life of persons of similar age and in particular shall include:

(a) Facilities for recreational and leisure activities;

(b) Facilities for education;

(c) Facilities to purchase or receive items for daily living, recreation and communication;

(d) Facilities, and encouragement to use such facilities, for a patient's engagement in active occupation suited to his or her social and cultural background, and for appropriate vocational rehabilitation measures to promote reintegration in the community. These measures should include vocational guidance, vocational training and placement services to enable patients to secure or retain employment in the community.

2.1. Are the living conditions in a mental health facility as close as possible to those of the normal life of persons of similar age?

2.2. What are the possibilities for recreational and leisure activities within the mental health facility?

2.3. What are the possibilities for education? Are there special requirements for the education of minors? (See Principle 2, §7., above.)

2.4. Can patients purchase or receive items for daily living, recreation and communication?

2.5. What are the possibilities provided for a patient's active occupation? Is the occupation suited to his/her social/cultural background?

2.6. Do guidelines exist to indicate the range of activities available to patients?

2.7. How is the patient encouraged to make use of such possibilities?

3. In no circumstances shall a patient be subject to forced labour. Within the limits compatible with the needs of the patient and with the requirements of institutional administration, a patient shall be able to choose the type of work he or she wishes to perform.

3.1. If a patient wishes to work, is he/she allowed to choose the kind of work to be performed?

3.2. Are patients subjected to forced and/or unpaid labour?

3.3. What remuneration does the patient receive for his/her work? What form does it take? [See Principle 1(4), §4.4., above.]

4. The labour of a patient in a mental health facility shall not be exploited. Every such patient shall have the right to receive the same remuneration for any work which he or she does as would, according to domestic law or custom, be paid for such work to a non-patient. Every such patient shall, in any event, have the right to receive a fair share of any remuneration which is paid to the mental health facility for his or her work.

4.1. What is done to promote reintegration into the community?

4.2. What are the measures taken for psychosocial rehabilitation?

4.3. Is there vocational guidance and training?

4.4. Are there placement services to enable patients to secure or retain employment in the community?

4.5. What linkage exists between mental health care facilities and:

— patients' employers?

— schools and other social agencies in the facility's area?

RESOURCES FOR MENTAL HEALTH FACILITIES

1. A mental health facility shall gave access to the same level of resources as any other health establishment, and in particular:

(a) Qualified medical and other appropriate professional staff in sufficient numbers and with adequate space to provide each patient with privacy and a programme of appropriate and active therapy;

(b) Diagnostic and therapeutic equipment for the patient;

(c) Appropriate professional care;

(d) Adequate, regular and comprehensive treatment, including supplies of medication.

1.1. What are the resources for the mental health facilities in comparison to those for other health facilities? What is the access for mental health treatment relative to treatment for physical disorders?

1.2. What is the staff member/patient ratio? (In general and in a given facility in particular)

1.3. Is there reasonable space for indicated treatment procedures, recreational activities and receiving visitors? (In general and in a given facility in particular)

1.4. Is each patient provided with privacy and a programme of appropriate and active therapy? (In general and in a given facility in particular)

1.5. Is funding for mental health services dependent, in any way, on political allegiance or persuasion?

1.6. Is funding for mental health services dependent, in any way, on religious belief or persuasion?

2. Every mental health facility shall be inspected by the competent authorities with sufficient frequency to ensure that the conditions, treatment and care of patients comply with the present principles.

2.1. By whom is the mental health facility inspected?

2.2. How frequently is the mental health facility inspected?

2.3. What are the accreditation requirements and procedures? What are the standards used? What are the consequences of accreditation or the lack thereof?

2.4. What percentage of institutions is denied accreditation?

PRINCIPLE 15

ADMISSION PRINCIPLES

1. Where a person needs treatment in a mental health facility, every effort shall be made to avoid involuntary admission.

1.1. Is there a voluntary admission procedure available and in use?

1.2. Are involuntary admissions avoided? If so, what is done to avoid involuntary admission?

1.3. What is the proportion of voluntary to involuntary admissions?

1.4. How often did involuntary admission happen recently (e.g. outpatient treatment, halfway houses, supportive apartments, partial hospitalizations)?

2. Access to a mental health facility shall be administered in the same way as access to any other facility for any other illness.

How is access to a mental health facility administered? What, if any, are the differences in administration for:

a. Voluntary vs. involuntary patients?

b. Insured vs. uninsured patients?

c. Public vs. general population patients?

d. Forensic vs. general population patients?

e. Violent vs. non-violent patients?

3. Every patient not admitted involuntarily shall have the right to leave the mental health facility at any time unless the criteria for his or her retention as an involuntary patient, as set forth in principle 16 below, apply, and he or she shall be informed of that right.

3.1. Is every voluntary patient free to leave the mental health facility at any time? What limitations are placed on this freedom? For example, if a patient wants to leave the grounds of the facility, must he/she request a pass? Are pass requests generally approved? If the patient wishes to discharge himself against medical advice, what is the procedure by which he may do so?

3.2. Is he/she informed of the right to request passes or to seek discharge, even against medical advice?

3.3. Under which circumstances is a patient not free to leave the mental health facility?

3.4. Are newly-arrived inpatients made to feel welcome on admission?

3.5. How are they informed about the main rules of the facility?

3.6. How are they informed of their rights? When are they informed of their rights? Are patients' rights listed and posted in a prominent place accessible to patients? (See also Principle 12, §1., above.)

3.7. Is the discharge plan discussed by all staff and with the patient concerned?

3.8. Whenever a patient is referred to another facility:

— is there a standard information form given to the patient?

— is such an information form sent to the facility?

3.9. What follow-up measures are taken? Are patients oriented in terms of other health and social services available in their communities?

3.10. Is medication adequately followed up — i.e. are prescriptions transferred? Are medical records transferred, particularly the medication records? Assuming a discharge to the community, is the patient aware of the procedure by and location from which he/she may obtain his/her medication? Is there direct contact between clinicians in the transmitting and the receiving facility? What, if any, are the fallback procedures?

INVOLUNTARY ADMISSION

1. A person may be admitted involuntarily to a mental health facility as a patient or, having already been admitted voluntarily as a patient, be retained as an involuntary patient in the mental health facility if, and only if, a qualified mental health practitioner authorized by law for that purpose determines, in accordance with principle 4 above, that person has a mental illness and considers:

(a) That, because of that mental illness, there is a serious likelihood of immediate or imminent harm to that person or to other persons; or

(b) That, in the case of a person whose mental illness is serve and whose judgement is impaired, failure to admit or retain that person is likely to lead to a serious deterioration in his or her condition or will prevent the giving of appropriate treatment that can only be given by admission to a mental health facility in accordance with the principle of the least restrictive alternative.

In the case referred to in subparagraph (b), a second such mental health practitioner, independent of the first, should be consulted where possible. If such consultation takes places, the involuntary admission or retention may not take place unless the second mental health practitioner concurs.

1.1. Who makes the decision on a person's involuntary admission?

1.2. What are the reasons for an involuntary admission?

1.3. Are second opinions required in order to authorize involuntary admission? If so, then

 — who chooses this second mental health practitioner?

 — is there a separate mental status examination?

 — are the two examinations held and documented separately?

 — does the second mental health practitioner have access to all records, or is such access deemed prejudicial?

1.4. Are the local laws drafted in such a way as to encourage involuntary admissions? For example, if a voluntary patient cannot be retained in the hospital as an involuntary patient, but rather must be discharged against medical advice and subsequently re-admitted on an involuntary basis, then, as a practical matter, the impetus is to admit on an involuntary basis initially, whether the status is justified or not.

2. Involuntary admission or retention shall initially be for a short period as specified by domestic law for observation and preliminary treatment pending review of the admission or retention by the review body. The grounds of the admission shall be communicated to the patient without delay and the fact of the admission and the grounds for it shall also be communicated promptly and in detail to the review body, to the patient's personal representative, if any, and, unless the patient objects, to the patient's family.

2.1. How long are patients retained involuntarily? Is this period of time determined, or limited, by statute?

2.2. Does the patient know the grounds of his/her admission?

2.3. Who else is informed of an involuntary admission? Is the patient's consent to this required? What is the procedure for minors who are involuntarily admitted? Are parents or guardians routinely informed?

3. A mental health facility may receive involuntarily admitted patients only if the facility has been designated to do so by a competent authority prescribed by domestic law.

3.1. Has the mental health facility receiving involuntary patients been designated by an authority competent to do so?

3.2. What is the competent authority to designate a mental health facility as appropriate to receive involuntary patients of specific classifications? For example, is the facility specifically designated as properly equipped to house and treat forensic patients?

REVIEW BODY

1. The review body shall be a judicial or other independent and impartial body established by domestic law and functioning in accordance with procedures laid down by domestic law. It shall, in formulating its decisions, have the assistance of one or more qualified and independent mental health practitioners and take their advice into account.

1.1. What is the nature of the body which reviews the involuntary admission or retention of a patient in a mental health facility?

1.2. What is the composition of this review body? Are members appointed, elected, hired? By whom?

1.3. Does the review body get any advice? From whom? In what form? For example, records' review, history, independent testimony?

1.4. How is this advice being applied?

2. The initial review of the review body, as required by paragraph 2 of Principle 16 above, of a decision to admit or retain a person as an involuntary patient shall take place as soon as possible after that decision and shall be conducted in accordance with simple and expeditious procedures as specified by domestic law.

What is the delay for an initial review after the decision to admit or retain a person?

3. The review body shall periodically review the cases of involuntary patients at reasonable intervals as specified by domestic law.

Is the review body bound to issue its decision within a specified time frame? If so, how long? If not, what is the typical time period in which the review body issues its decision?

4. An involuntary patient may apply to the review body for release or voluntary status, at reasonable intervals as specified by domestic law.

At what intervals does the patient have the right to apply to the review body for release or voluntary status?

5. At each review, the review body shall consider whether the criteria for involuntary admission set out in paragraph 1 of principle 16 above are still satisfied, and, if not, the patient shall be discharged as an involuntary patient.

Under what conditions will the patient be discharged?

6. If at any time the mental health practitioner responsible for the

case is satisfied that the conditions for the retention of a person as an involuntary patient are no longer satisfied, he or she shall order the discharge of that person as such a patient.

6.1. Are mental health care providers required, by local law, to change the patient's status from involuntary to voluntary should the underlying conditions which justified the involuntary retention no longer be satisfied?
6.2. Are mental health care providers allowed by local law, to change the patient's status from involuntary to voluntary should the underlying conditions which justified the involuntary retention no longer be satisfied?

7. A patient or his personal representative or any interested person shall have the right to appeal to a higher court against a decision that the patient be admitted to, or be retained in, a mental health facility.

7.1. Do patients or their guardians have the right to appeal the decision on admission to or retention in a mental health facility?

PROCEDURAL SAFEGUARDS

1. The patient shall be entitled to choose and appoint a counsel to represent the patient as such, including representation in any complaint procedure or appeal. If the patient does not secure such services, a counsel shall be made available without payment by the patient to the extent that the patient lacks sufficient means to pay.

1.1. How is the patient represented in any complaint procedure or appeal?

1.2. How is this representation financed?

2. The patient shall also be entitled to the assistance, if necessary, of the services of an interpreter. Where such services are necessary and the patient does not secure them, they shall be made available without payment by the patient to the extent that the patient lacks sufficient means to pay.

2.1. If a patient does not have an adequate command of the official language of the court, will the services of an interpreter be made available to the patient, without payment if necessary?

3. The patient and the patient's counsel may request and produce at any hearing an independent mental health report and any other

reports and oral, written and other evidence that are relevant and admissible.

3.1. Does the patient or his/her counsel have the right to request at any hearing an independent mental health report and other reports together with oral, written and other evidence? Who would pay for this independent assessment?

4. Copies of the patient's records and any reports and documents to be submitted shall be given to the patient and to the patient's counsel, except in special cases where it is determined that a specific disclosure to the patient would cause serious harm to the patient's health or put at risk the safety of others. As domestic law may provide, any document not given to the patient should, when this can be done in confidence, be given to the patient's personal representative and counsel. When any part of a document is withheld from a patient, the patient or the patient's counsel, if any, shall receive notice of the withholding and the reasons for it and it shall be subject to judicial review.

4.1. Are copies of the patient's records (and any reports and documents to be submitted) given to the patient and to the patient's counsel as a matter of course?

4.2. If not, why?

4.3. If yes, when? Is the documentation provided sufficiently in advance of the hearing to provide adequate opportunity for review?

4.4. Is any document which is not given to the patient given to the patient's personal representative and counsel? If so, under what circumstances?

4.5. In case of withholding a document or part of a document, will the patient be informed?

4.6. Who else will be informed?

4.7. Are the reasons for this withholding given?

4.8. Is this withholding subject to a judicial review?

5. The patient and the patient's personal representative and counsel shall be entitled to attend, participate and be heard personally in any hearing.

5.1. Does the patient have the right to attend, participate and be heard in meaningful manner in any hearing?

5.2. Who else has this right?

5.3. Does the patient have the right to produce any evidence at any hearing?

6. If the patient or the patient's personal representative or counsel requests that a particular person be present at a hearing, that person shall be admitted unless it is determined that the person's presence could cause serious harm to the patient's health or put at risk the safety of others.

6.1. Who may be present at a hearing?

6.2. Who appoints the persons present at a hearing?

6.3. Is the patient's request for the presence of a particular person at a hearing respected?

6.4. Who else is entitled to make such a request and will such a request be respected? If not, why?

7. Any decision on whether the hearing or any part of it shall be in public or in private and may be publicly reported shall give full consideration to the patient's own wishes, to the need to respect the privacy of the patient and of other persons and to the need to prevent serious harm to the patient's health or to avoid putting at risk the safety of others.

7.1. What are the rights of a patient in a hearing? Is the hearing public or private?

7.2. Who decides on this issue?

7.3. Is the patient's privacy respected and confidentiality maintained?

7.4. Is the privacy of other parties respected?

7.5. What are the personal representative's and the counsel's rights?

7.6. How is the patient of his/her representative informed about these rights?

8. The decision arising out of the hearing and the reasons for it shall be expressed in writing. Copies shall be given to the patient and his or her personal representative and counsel. In deciding whether the decision shall be published in whole or in part, full

consideration shall be given to the patient's own wishes, to the need to respect his or her privacy and that of other persons, to the public interest in the open administration of justice and to the need to prevent serious harm to the patient's health or to avoid putting at risk the safety of others.

8.1. In what form is the decision arising out of the hearing expressed?

8.2. How are the reasons for the decision given?

8.3. Who decides on the publication of the decision?

8.4. Does the patient receive copies of the judgment?

8.5. What is done to prevent intimidation of the patient?

8.6. What is done to make the patient feel at ease?

ACCESS TO INFORMATION

1. A patient (which term in the present Principle includes a former patient) shall be entitled to have access to the information concerning the patient in his or her health and personal records maintained by a mental health facility. This right may be subject to restriction in order to prevent serious harm to the patient's health and avoid putting at risk the safety of others. As domestic law may provide, any such information not given to the patient should, when this can be done in confidence, be given to the patient's personal representative and counsel. When any of the information is withheld from a patient, the patient or the patient's counsel, if any, shall receive notice of the withholding and the reasons for it and it shall be subject to judicial review.

1.1. Can patients access their medical records upon request?

1.2. If not, why is this information withheld?

1.3. If any information is withheld from the patient, who will receive notice of this?

1.4. If not given to the patient, to whom, if anyone, is any such information given?

1.5. Do patients review their records with a mental health practitioner, or independently?

1.6. If any information is withheld from the patient, what sort of judicial procedure, if any, will result?

2. Any written comments by the patient or the patient's personal representative or counsel shall, on request, be inserted in the patient's file.

2.1. What information does the patient's record include?

2.2. Is information recorded in a legible format and does it ensure full confidentiality?

2.3. May the patient or his personal representative insert comments or other documentation into his own record, provided he/she does not alter the existing record?

CRIMINAL OFFENDERS

1. The present Principle applies to persons serving sentences of imprisonment for criminal offences, or who are otherwise detained in the course of criminal proceedings or investigations against them, and who are determined to have a mental illness or who it is believed may have such an illness.

1.1. Who is considered a criminal offender?

1.2. Is there a status for those deemed not guilty by reason of insanity (NGRI)?

1.3. If so, what are the specific procedures for those deemed to be NGRI?

1.4. What about mentally in persons out on bond? Can they be forced to seek treatment as a condition to their freedom? How is this treatment verified? Is there an adequate parole function so that orders for treatment are followed?

2. All such persons should receive the best available mental health care as provided in Principle I above. The present Principles shall apply to them to the fullest extent possible, with only such limited modifications and exceptions as are necessary in the circumstances. No such modifications and exceptions shall prejudice the person's rights under the instrument noted in paragraph 5 of Principle 1 above.

2.1. Within the prison system, what is the nature of the health care for prisoners?

2.2. Is health care guaranteed to prisoners?

2.3. Is there a hospital section within each individual prison?

2.4. Is mental health care guaranteed to prisoners?

2.5. Is there a specific forensic hospital in which mentally-ill prisoners a treated locally?

2.6. Are mentally-ill patients kept with the general prison population, or are they placed in private or semi-private cells or within the hospital section of the prison, assuming one exists?

3. Domestic law may authorize a court or other competent authority, acting on the basis of competent and independent medical advice, to order that such persons be admitted to a mental health facility.

3.1. May prisoners be admitted to mental health facilities?

3.2. If so, which ones, and for what purpose?

  a. Restoration to competency? Before or after trial?

  b. As part of sentencing? May part or all of the sentence be served within the mental health facility?

3.3. If the answer to 3.1. above is "yes", by whom may they be admitted?

3.4. Is the prisoner's right to informed consent to treatment respected in any case? How is the voluntariness of treatment safeguarded in light of restoration to competency to stand trial? For example, if the prisoner is deemed not competent but restorable, may he refuse the treatment which it is assumed would restore him to competence?

4. Treatment of persons determined to have a mental illness shall in all circumstances be consistent with principle 11 above.

4.1. What are the special safeguards regarding the personal integrity of the mentally disordered prisoner, particularly with regard to limits on personal restraint privacy?

4.2. Are the guards and prison officials trained to be aware of the basic symptoms of mental disorders?

4.3. Are the guards and prison officials trained to be sensitive to the needs of those with a mental disorder?

4.4. Are people with mental disorders disproportionately represented in the local prison system? Given that there is co-morbidity that exists naturally, are local ratios disproportionate to the representation of the mentally ill in other places? In other words, is mental disorder, in effect, being criminalized?

4.5. Is the prison system, as opposed to the health care system. being used to house and protect mentally-ill people?

PRINCIPLE 21

COMPLAINTS

Every patient and former patient shall have the right to make a complaint through procedures as specified by domestic law.

1. What procedures exist by which a patient may make a complaint about his experience in the mental health system?

2. Are there written procedures available for dealing with complaints from patients and facilities?

3. Is submission, investigation and resolution of complaints guaranteed?

4. What level of authority deals with complaints?

5. Is there a follow up procedure whereby cases are reviewed in order to safeguard against retribution towards patients for filing complaints?

MONITORING AND REMEDIES

States shall ensure that appropriate mechanisms are in force to promote compliance with the present Principles, for the inspection of mental health facilities, for the submission, investigation and resolution of complaints and for the institution of appropriate disciplinary or judicial proceedings for professional misconduct or violation of the rights of a patient.

1. What is done by the state to promote compliance with the present principles?

2. Is there an inspection scheme for mental health facilities?

3. What is the procedure in case of professional misconduct or violation of the rights of a patient?

4. Does compliance with the present principles affect accreditation or professional licences?

5. What are the consequences of lack of compliance? For example, can facilities be closed, denied reimbursement by third party payers or placed under guardianship?

6. Are there criminal penalties as well as administrative ones available? Are they enforced?

7. Are intra- and international records kept and cross-indexed so that a person deemed to have been abusive of or negligent toward a mental patient does not simply enter another state or province or obtain another license to practice?

IMPLEMENTATION

1. States should implement the present Principles through appropriate legislative, judicial, administrative, educational and other measures, which they shall review periodically.

1.1. What measures (legislative, judicial, administrative, educational and others) are taken to implement the present principles?

1.2. How frequently are these measures reviewed?

1.3. Is there a strategy to ensure implementation and continued adequate enforcement of the present principles?

1.4. How is mental health promoted?

1.5. Who participates in the preparation and maintenance of mental health programmes?

1.6. Is there a specific governmental body whose task it is to promote and maintain quality of mental health treatment?

2. States shall make the present Principles widely known by appropriate and active means.

2.1. How are the Principles disseminated?

2.2. Is there a dissemination strategy?

2.3. Are the contents of the Principles made known in laymen's terms?

2.4. Are the contents of these Principles made known in any local language?

PRINCIPLE 24

SCOPE OF PRINCIPLES RELATING TO MENTAL HEALTH FACILITIES

The present Principles apply to all persons who are admitted to a mental health facility.

1. Do the present Principles apply to all persons who are admitted to mental health facilities?

2. If not, to which types of patients are the present Principles inapplicable, when, under what circumstances, for how long, etc.?

SAVING OF EXISTING RIGHTS

There shall be no restriction upon or derogation from any existing rights of patients, including rights recognized in applicable international or domestic law, on the pretext that the present Principles do not recognize such rights or that they recognize them to a lesser extent.

1. Are these Principles seen as a minimum standard or threshold to be met in terms of the rights of the mentally ill, or are they seen as a ceiling?

2. Has the enactment of the present Principles served in any way to limit, restrict, or lower the standards of the rights and treatment of the mentally ill?

Part 2

Checklist

Checklist

	YES	NO
1. Can persons with mental disorders exercise their civil, economic and cultural rights, e.g.		
1.1. the right to marry.		
1.2. the right to own property.		
1.3. the right to vote.		
1.4. the right to have children and to maintain parental rights.		
1.5. the right to access to one's own medical records.		
1.6. the right to freedom cruel, inhuman or degrading treatment or punishment?		
2. Are there laws prohibiting discrimination against persons with a mental disorder? If YES, please, specify:		
3. Is there legislation governing mental health care? If YES, please, specify:		
4. Is there legislation governing the commitment of patients (to treatment and/or to admission)? If YES, please, specify:		
5. Is there a specific government body responsible for promoting and maintaining the quality of mental health care? If YES, please, specify:		
6. Are there provisions for education for minors with mental disorders? If YES, please, specify:		
7. Are there standards for the determination of mental disorders (e.g. ICD; DSM)? If YES, please, specify:		

8. Are the standards of care for people with mental disorders comparable to those for physically ill persons?		
9. Are the resources (human, financial and material) for mental health facilities comparable to those for other health facilities?		
10. Are patients always asked for an informed consent prior to the beginning of a treatment?		
11. Are there forms of restraint which are allowed and which are not? If YES, please, specify:		
12. Does use of drug therapy follow internationally accepted guidelines for mental disorders? If YES, please, specify:		
13. Are there essential drugs widely available (e.g. within one hour's walk for all patients) for the treatment of mental disorders? Please, specify:		
14. Is there an operational system to protect confidentiality? If YES, please, specify:		
15. Can patients access their medical records upon request?		
16. Is a patient treated in a mental health facility always informed of his/her rights?		
17. Is there a voluntary commitment?		
18. Is there a time limit on involuntary commitment? If YES, please, specify:		
19. Do patients have the right to appeal a decision on involuntary admission? If YES, please, specify:		

20. Is the patient represented in any complaint procedure or appeal? If YES, please, specify:		
21. Are there living arrangements (both in institutions and in the community) tailored to the needs of those with mental disorders? If YES, please, specify:		
22. Are there specific programmes or measures taken for psychosocial rehabilitation? If YES, please, specify:		
23. Are prisons or jails being used to house people with mental disorders?		
24. Is there a specific forensic hospital for mentally-ill prisoners?		
25. Is mental health care guaranteed to prisoners?		
26. How far away from home is the majority or patients being treated?		
27. What is the average duration of an inpatient psychiatric hospitalization?		
28. What is the proportion of voluntary to involuntary admissions?		
29. How many signatures (and of whom?) are required for involuntarily commitment?		
30. What authority reviews involuntary admissions?		

Universal Declaration of Human Rights[*]

PREAMBLE

Whereas recognition of the inherent dignity and of the equal and inalienable rights of all members of the human family is the foundation of freedom, justice and peace in the world,

Whereas disregard and contempt for human rights have resulted in barbarous acts which have outraged the conscience of mankind, and the advent of a world in which human beings shall enjoy freedom of speech and belief and freedom from fear and want has been proclaimed as the highest aspiration of the common people,

Whereas it is essential, if man is not to be compelled to have recourse, as a last resort, to rebellion against tyranny and oppression, that human rights should be protected by the rule of law,

Whereas it is essential to promote the development of friendly relations between nations,

Whereas the peoples of the United Nations have in the Charter reaffirmed their faith in fundamental human rights, in the dignity and worth of the human person and in the equal rights of men and women and have determined to promote social progress and better standards of life in larger freedom,

---

[*] 유네스코 한국위원회 국제인권조약집(http://www.unesco.or.kr/hrtreaty/)

Whereas Member States have pledged themselves to achieve, in cooperation with the United Nations, the promotion of universal respect for and observance of human rights and fundamental freedoms,

Whereas a common understanding of these rights and freedoms is of the greatest importance for the full realization of this pledge,

Now, therefore, The General Assembly, Proclaims this Universal Declaration of Human Rights as a common standard of achievement for all peoples and all nations, to the end that every individual and every organ of society, keeping this Declaration constantly in mind, shall strive by teaching and education to promote respect for these rights and freedoms and by progressive measures, national and international, to secure their universal and effective recognition and observance, both among the peoples of Member States themselves and among the peoples of territories under their jurisdiction.

Article 1

All human beings are born free and equal in dignity and rights. They are endowed with reason and conscience and should act towards one another in a spirit of brotherhood.

Article 2

Everyone is entitled to all the rights and freedoms set forth in this Declaration, without distinction of any kind, such as race, colour, sex, language, religion, political or other opinion, national or social origin, property, birth or other status.

Furthermore, no distinction shall be made on the basis of the political, jurisdictional or international status of the country or territory to which a person belongs, whether it be independent, trust, non-self-governing or under any other limitation of sovereignty.

Article 3

Everyone has the right to life, liberty and security of person.

Article 4

No one shall be held in slavery or servitude; slavery and the slave trade shall be prohibited in all their forms.

Article 5

No one shall be subjected to torture or to cruel, inhuman or degrading treatment or punishment.

Article 6

Everyone has the right to recognition everywhere as a person before the law.

Article 7

All are equal before the law and are entitled without any discrimination to equal protection of the law. All are entitled to equal protection against any discrimination in violation of this Declaration and against any incitement to such discrimination.

Article 8

Everyone has the right to an effective remedy by the competent national tribunals for acts violating the fundamental rights granted him by the constitution or by law.

Article 9

No one shall be subjected to arbitrary arrest, detention or exile.

Article 10

Everyone is entitled in full equality to a fair and public hearing by an independent and impartial tribunal, in the determination of his rights and obligations and of any criminal charge against him.

Article 11

1. Everyone charged with a penal offence has the right to be presumed innocent until proved guilty according to law in a public trial at which he has had all the guarantees necessary for his defence.

2. No one shall be held guilty of any penal offence on account of any act or omission which did not constitute a penal offence, under national or international law, at the time when it was committed. Nor shall a heavier penalty be imposed than the one that was applicable at the time the penal offence was committed.

Article 12

No one shall be subjected to arbitrary interference with his privacy, family, home or correspondence, nor to attacks upon his honour and reputation. Everyone has the right to the protection of the law against such interference or attacks.

Article 13

1. Everyone has the right to freedom of movement and residence within the borders of each State.

2. Everyone has the right to leave any country, including his own, and to return to his country.

Article 14

1. Everyone has the right to seek and to enjoy in other countries asylum from persecution.

2. This right may not be invoked in the case of prosecutions genuinely arising from non-political crimes or from acts contrary to the purposes and principles of the United Nations.

Article 15

1. Everyone has the right to a nationality.

2. No one shall be arbitrarily deprived of his nationality nor denied the right to change his nationality.

Article 16

1. Men and women of full age, without any limitation due to race, nationality or religion, have the right to marry and to found a family. They are entitled

to equal rights as to marriage, during marriage and at its dissolution.

2. Marriage shall be entered into only with the free and full consent of the intending spouses.

3. The family is the natural and fundamental group unit of society and is entitled to protection by society and the State.

Article 17

1. Everyone has the right to own property alone as well as in association with others.

2. No one shall be arbitrarily deprived of his property.

Article 18

Everyone has the right to freedom of thought, conscience and religion; this right includes freedom to change his religion or belief, and freedom, either alone or in community with others and in public or private, to manifest his religion or belief in teaching, practice, worship and observance.

Article 19

Everyone has the right to freedom of opinion and expression; this right includes freedom to hold opinions without interference and to seek, receive and impart information and ideas through any media and regardless of frontiers.

Article 20

1. Everyone has the right to freedom of peaceful assembly and association.

2. No one may be compelled to belong to an association.

Article 21

1. Everyone has the right to take part in the government of his country, directly or through freely chosen representatives.

2. Everyone has the right to equal access to public service in his country.

3. The will of the people shall be the basis of the authority of government; this will shall be expressed in periodic and genuine elections which shall be by universal and equal suffrage and shall be held by secret vote or by equivalent free voting procedures.

Article 22

Everyone, as a member of society, has the right to social security and is entitled to realization, through national effort and international co-operation and in accordance with the organization and resources of each State, of the economic, social and cultural rights indispensable for his dignity and the free development of his personality.

Article 23

1. Everyone has the right to work, to free choice of employment, to just and favourable conditions of work and to protection against unemployment.

2. Everyone, without any discrimination, has the right to equal pay for equal work.

3. Everyone who works has the right to just and favourable remuneration ensuring for himself and his family an existence worthy of human dignity,

and supplemented, if necessary, by other means of social protection.

4. Everyone has the right to form and to join trade unions for the protection of his interests.

Article 24

Everyone has the right to rest and leisure, including reasonable limitation of working hours and periodic holidays with pay.

Article 25

1. Everyone has the right to a standard of living adequate for the health and well-being of himself and of his family, including food, clothing, housing and medical care and necessary social services, and the right to security in the event of unemployment, sickness, disability, widowhood, old age or other lack of livelihood in circumstances beyond his control.

2. Motherhood and childhood are entitled to special care and assistance. All children, whether born in or out of wedlock, shall enjoy the same social protection.

Article 26

1. Everyone has the right to education. Education shall be free, at least in the elementary and fundamental stages. Elementary education shall be compulsory. Technical and professional education shall be made generally available and higher education shall be equally accessible to all on the basis of merit.

2. Education shall be directed to the full development of the human personality

and to the strengthening of respect for human rights and fundamental freedoms. It shall promote understanding, tolerance and friendship among all nations, racial or religious groups, and shall further the activities of the United Nations for the maintenance of peace.

3. Parents have a prior right to choose the kind of education that shall be given to their children.

Article 27

1. Everyone has the right freely to participate in the cultural life of the community, to enjoy the arts and to share in scientific advancement and its benefits.

2. Everyone has the right to the protection of the moral and material interests resulting from any scientific, literary or artistic production of which he is the author.

Article 28

Everyone is entitled to a social and international order in which the rights and freedoms set forth in this Declaration can be fully realized.

Article 29

1. Everyone has duties to the community in which alone the free and full development of his personality is possible.

2. In the exercise of his rights and freedoms, everyone shall be subject only to such limitations as are determined by law solely for the purpose of securing due recognition and respect for the rights and freedoms of others and of meeting

the just requirements of morality, public order and the general welfare in a democratic society.

3. These rights and freedoms may in no case be exercised contrary to the purposes and principles of the United Nations.

Article 30

Nothing in this Declaration may be interpreted as implying for any State, group or person any right to engage in any activity or to perform any act aimed at the destruction of any of the rights and freedoms set forth herein.

Declaration on the Rights of Disabled Persons

Proclaimed by General Assembly Resolution 3447(XXX) of 9 December 1975

The General Assembly,

Mindful of the pledge mad by Member States, under the Charter of the United Nations to take joint and separate action in co-operation with the Organization to promote higher standards of living, full employment and conditions of economic and social progress and development,

Reaffirming its faith in human rights and fundamental freedoms and in the principles of peace, of the dignity and worth of the human person and of social justice proclaimed in the Charter,

Recalling the principles of the Universal Declaration of Human Rights, the International Covenants on Human Rights, the Declaration of the Rights of the Child and the Declaration on the Rights of Mentally Retarded Persons, as well as the standards already set for social progress in the constitutions, conventions, recommendations and resolutions of the International Labour Organization, the United Nations Educational, Scientific and Cultural Organization, the World Health Organization, the United Nations Children's Fund and other organizations concerned,

Recalling also Economic and Social Council resolution 1921(LVIII) of 6 May 1975 on the prevention of disability and the rehabilitation of disabled persons,

Emphasizing that the Declaration on Social Progress and Development has proclaimed the necessity of protecting the rights and assuring the welfare and rehabilitation of the physically and mentally disadvantaged,

Bearing in mind the necessity of preventing physical and mental disabilities of assisting disabled persons to develop their abilities in the most varied fields of activities and of promoting their integration as far as possible in normal life,

Aware that certain countries, at their present stage of development, can devote only limited efforts to this end,

Proclaims this Declaration on the Rights of Disabled Persons and calls for national and international action to ensure that it will be used as a common basis and frame of reference for the protection of these rights:

1. The term "disabled person" means any person unable to ensure by himself or herself, wholly or partly, the necessities of a normal individual and/or social life, as a result of deficiency, either congenital or not, in his or her physical or mental capabilities.

2. Disabled persons shall enjoy all the rights set forth in this Declaration. These rights shall be granted to all disabled persons without any exception whatsoever and without distinction or discrimination on the basis of race, colour, sex, language, religion, political or other opinions, national or social origin, state of wealth, birth or any other situation applying either to the disabled person himself or herself or to his or her family.

3. Disabled persons have the inherent right to respect for their human dignity.

Disabled persons, whatever the origin, nature and seriousness of their handicaps and disabilities, have the same fundamental rights as their fellow-citizens of the same age, which implies first and foremost the right to enjoy a decent life, as normal and full as possible.

4. Disabled persons have the same civil and political rights as other human beings; paragraph 7 of the Declaration on the Rights of Mentally Retarded Persons applies to any possible limitation or suppression or those rights for mentally disabled persons.

5. Disabled persons are entitled to the measures designed to enable them to become as self-reliant as possible.

6. Disabled persons have the right to medical, psychological and functional treatment, including prosthetic and orthotic appliances, to medical and social rehabilitation, education, vocational training and rehabilitation, aid, counselling, placement services and other services which will enable them to develop their capabilities and skills to the maximum and will hasten the processes of their social integration or reintegration.

7. Disabled persons have the right to economic and social security and to a decent level of living. They have the right, according to their capabilities, to secure and retain employment or to engage in a useful, productive and remunerative occupation and to join trade unions.

8. Disabled persons are entitled to have their special needs taken into consideration at all stages of economic and social planning.

9. Disabled persons have the right to live with their families or with foster parents and to participate in all social, creative or recreational activities. No disabled person shall be subjected, as far as his or her residence is concerned, to differential treatment other than that required by his or her condition or by the improvement which he or she may derive therefrom. If the stay of a disabled person in a specialized establishment is indispensable, the environment and living conditions therein shall be as close as possible to those of the normal life of a person of his or her age.

10. Disabled persons shall be protected against all exploitation, all regulations and all treatment of a discriminatory, abusive or degrading nature.

11. Disabled persons shall be able to avail themselves of qualified legal aid when such aid proves indispensable for the protection of their persons and property. If judicial proceedings are instituted against them, the legal procedure applied shall take their physical and mental condition fully into account.

12. Organizations of disabled persons may be usefully consulted in all matters regarding the rights of disabled persons.

13. Disabled persons, their families and communities shall be fully informed, by all appropriate means, of the rights contained in this Declaration.

Declaration on the Rights
of Mentally Retarded Persons

Proclaimed by General Assembly Resolution 2856(XXVI) of 20 December 1971

The General Assembly,

Mindful of the pledge of the States Members of the United Nations under the Charter to take joint and separate action in co-operation with the organization to promote higher standards of living, full employment and conditions of economic and social progress and development,

Reaffirming faith in human rights and fundamental freedoms and in the principles of peace, of the dignity and worth of the human person and of social justice proclaimed in the Charter,

Recalling the principles of the Universal Declaration of Human Rights, the International Covenants on Human Rights, the Declaration of the Rights of the Child and the standards already set for social progress in the constitutions, conventions, recommendations and resolutions of the International Labour Organization, the United Nations Educational, Scientific and Cultural Organization, the World Health Organization, the United Nations Children's Fund and other organizations concerned,

Emphasizing that the Declaration on Social Progress and Development has proclaimed the necessity of protecting the rights and assuring the welfare and rehabilitation of the physically and mentally disadvantaged,

Bearing in mind the necessity of assisting mentally retarded persons to develop their abilities in various fields of activities and of promoting their integration as far as possible in normal life,

Aware that certain countries, at their present stage of development, can devote only limited efforts to this end,

Proclaims this Declaration on the Rights of Mentally Retarded Persons and calls for national and international action to ensure that it will be used as a common basis and frame of reference for the protection of these rights:

1. The mentally retarded person has, to the maximum degree of feasibility, the same rights as other human beings.

2. The mentally retarded person has a right to proper medical care and physical therapy and to such education, training, rehabilitation and guidance as will enable him to develop his ability and maximum potential.

3. The mentally retarded person has a right to economic security and to a decent standard of living. He has a right to perform productive work or to engage in any other meaningful occupation to the fullest possible extent of his capabilities.

4. Whenever possible, the mentally retarded person should live with his own family or with foster parents and participate in different forms of community life. The family with which he lives should receive assistance. If care in an institution becomes necessary, it should be provided in surroundings and other circumstances as close as possible to those of normal life.

5. The mentally retarded person has a right to a qualified guardian when this is required to protect his personal well-being and interests.

6. The mentally retarded person has a right to protection from exploitation, abuse and degrading treatment. If prosecuted for any offence, he shall have a right to due process of law with full recognition being given to his degree of mental responsibility.

7. Whenever mentally retarded persons are unable, because of the severity of their handicap, to exercise all their rights in a meaningful way or it should become necessary to restrict to deny some or all of these rights, the procedure used for that restriction or denial of rights must contain proper legal safeguards against every form of abuse. This procedure must be based on an evaluation of the social capability of the mentally retarded person by qualified experts and must be subject to periodic review and to the right of appeal to higher authorities.

Declaration of Caracas

The following Declaration was adopted by acclamation on 14 November 1990 by the Regional Conference on Restructuring Psychiatric care in Latin America, which was held in Caracas, 11~14 November 1990, under the auspices of the Pan American Health Organization/WHO Regional Office for the Americas:

The legislators, associations, health authorities, mental health professionals, and jurists assembled at the Regional Conference on the Restructuring of Psychiatric Care in Latin America within the Local health Systems Model,

Noting,

1. That conventional psychiatric services do not allow for attainment of the objectives entailed in community-based care that is decentralized, participatory, integrated, continuing, and preventive;

2. That the mental hospital, when it is the only form of psychiatric care provided, hampers fulfilment of the foregoing objectives in that it:

   (a) isolates patients from their natural environment, thus generating greater social disability;

   (b) creates unfavourable conditions that imperil the human and civil rights of patients;

   (c) absorbs the bulk of financial and human resources allotted by the countries for mental health care;

(d) fails to provide professional training that is adequately geared to the mental health needs of the population, the general health services, and other sectors.

Considering,

1. That Primary Health Care is the strategy that has been adopted by WHO and PAHO and endorsed by all the Members States as the means for attaining the goal of Health for all by the Year 2000;

2. That the Local Health Systems model has been implemented by the countries of this Region as the means for reaching that target through the provision of better conditions for the development of programs that are based on the health needs of the population and that emphasize decentralization, social participation, and the preventive approach;

3. That mental health and psychiatric programs must incorporate the principles and guidelines on which these strategies and models of health care delivery are based,

DECLARE

1. That the restructuring of psychiatric care on the basis of Primary Health Care and within the framework of the Local Health Systems model will permit the promotion of alternative service models that are community-based and

integrated into social and health networks.

2. That the restructuring of psychiatric care in the Region implies a critical review of the dominant and centralizing role played by the mental hospital in mental health service delivery.

3. That the resources, care, and treatment that are made available must:
   (a) safeguard personal dignity and human and civil rights;
   (b) be based on criteria that are rational and technically appropriate; and
   (c) strive to ensure that patients remain in their communities.

4. That national legislation must be redrafted if necessary so that:
   (a) the human and civil rights of mental patients are safeguarded; and
   (b) that the organization of the services guarantees the enforcement of these rights.

5. That training in mental health and psychiatry should use a service model that is based on the community health center and encourages psychiatric admissions in general hospitals, in accordance with the principles that underlie the restructuring movement.

6. That the organizations, associations, and other participants in this Conference hereby undertake to advocate and develop programs at the country level that will promote the restructuring desired, and at the same time that they commit themselves to monitoring and defending the human rights of mental patients

in accordance with national legislation and international agreements.

To this end, they call upon the Ministries of Health and Justice, the Parliaments, Social Security and other care-providing institutions, professional organizations, consumer associations, universities and other training facilities, and the media to support the restructuring of psychiatric care, thus assuring its successful development for the benefit of the population in the Region.

Declaration of Hawaii/II

As approved in 1992 by the General Assembly of the World Psychiatric Association

Ever since the dawn of culture, ethics has been an essential part of the healing art. It is the view of the World Psychiatric Association that due to conflicting loyalties and expectations of both physicians and patients in contemporary society and the delicate nature of the therapist-patient relationship, high ethical standards are specially important for those involved in the science and practice of psychiatry as a medical speciality. These guidelines have been delineated in order to promote close adherence to those standards and to prevent misuse of psychiatric concepts, knowledge and technology.

Since the psychiatrist is a member of society as well as a practitioner of medicine, he or she must consider the ethical implications specific to psychiatry as well as the ethical demands on all physicians and the societal responsibility of every man and woman.

Even though ethical behaviour is based on the individual psychiatrist's conscience and personal judgement, written guidelines are needed to clarify the profession's ethical implication.

Therefore, the General Assembly of the world Psychiatric Association has approved these ethical guidelines for psychiatrists, having in mind the great differences in cultural backgrounds, and in legal, social and economic conditions which exist in the various countries of the world. It should be understood that the World Psychiatric Association views these guidelines to be minimal requirements for ethical standards of the psychiatric profession.

1. The aim of psychiatry is to treat mental illness and to promote mental health to the best of his or her ability, consistent with accepted scientific knowledge and ethical principles, the psychiatrist shall serve the best interests of the patient and be also concerned for the common good and a just allocation of health resources. To fulfill these aims requires continuous research and continual education of health care personnel, patients and public.

2. Every psychiatrist should offer to the patient the best available therapy to his knowledge and if accepted must treat him or her with the solicitude and respect due to the dignity of all human beings. When the psychiatrist is responsible for treatment given by others he owes them competent supervision and education. Whenever there is a need, or whenever a reasonable request is forthcoming from the patient, the psychiatrist should seek the help of another colleague.

3. The psychiatrist aspires for a therapeutic relationship that is founded on mutual agreement. At its optimum it requires trust, confidentiality, cooperation and mutual responsibility. Such a relationship may not be possible to establish with some patients. In that case, contact should be established with a relative or other person close to the patient. If and when a relationship is established for purposes other than therapeutic, such as in forensic psychiatry, its nature must be thoroughly explained to the person concerned.

4. The psychiatrist should inform the patient of the nature of the condition, therapeutic procedures, including possible alternatives, and of the possible outcome. This information must be offered in a considerate way and the patient must be given the opportunity to choose between appropriate and available methods.

5. No procedure shall be performed nor treatment given against or independent of a patient's own will, unless because of mental illness, the patient cannot form a judgement as so what is in his of her own best interest and without which treatment serious impairment is likely to occur to the patient or others.

6. As soon as the conditions for compulsory treatment no longer apply, the psychiatrist should release the patient from the compulsory nature of the treatment and if further therapy is necessary should obtain voluntary consent. The psychiatrists should inform the patient and/or relatives or meaningful others, of the existence of mechanisms of appeal for the detention and for any other complaints related to his of her well being.

7. The psychiatrist must never use his professional possibilities to violate the dignity of human rights of any individual or group and should never let inappropriate personal desire, feelings, prejudices or beliefs interfere with the treatment. The psychiatrist must on no account utilize the tools of his profession, once the absence of psychiatric illness has been established. If a patient or some third party demands actions contrary to scientific knowledge or ethical principles the psychiatrist must refuse to cooperate.

8. Whatever the psychiatrist has been told by the patient, or has noted during examination or treatment, must be kept confidential unless the patient relieves the psychiatrist from this obligation, or to prevent serious harm to self or others makes disclosure necessary, in these cases, however, the patient should be informed of the breach of confidentiality.

9. To increase and propagate psychiatric knowledge and skill requires participation of the patients. Informed consent must, however, be obtained presenting a patient to a class and, if possible, also when a case-history is released for scientific publication, whereby all reasonable measures must be taken to preserve the dignity and anonymity of the patients and to safeguard the personal reputation of the subject. The patient's participation must be voluntary, after full information has been given of the aim, procedures, risks and inconveniences of a research project and three must always be a reasonable relationship between calculated risks or inconveniences and the benefit of the study. In clinical research every subject must retain and exert all high rights as a patient. For children and other patients who cannot themselves give informed consent, this should be obtained from the legal next-of-kin. Every patient or research subject is free to withdraw for any reason at any time from any voluntary treatment and from any teaching or research program in which he or she participates. This withdrawal, as well as any refusal to enter a program, must never influence the psychiatrist's efforts to help the patient or subject.

10. The psychiatrist should stop all therapeutic, teaching or research program that may evolve contrary to the principles of this Declaration.

Recommendation 1235(1994)
on Psychiatry and Human Rights

Parliamentary Assembly of the Council of Europe – 1994 Session

1. The Assembly observes that there is no overall study on legislation and practice with regard to psychiatry covering the member states of the Council of Europe.

2. It notes that on the one hand, a body of case-law has developed on the basis of the European Convention on Human Rights and that on the other, the European Committee for the Prevention of Torture and Inhuman or Degrading Treatment or Punishment has made a number of observations with regard to practices followed in the matter of psychiatric placements.

3. It notes that, in a large number of member countries, legislation on psychiatry is under review or in preparation.

4. It is aware that, in many countries, a lively debate is currently focused on problems associated with certain types of treatment such as lobotomies and electroconvulsive therapy as well as on sexual abuse in psychiatric care.

5. It recalls Recommendation No. R(83)2 of the Committee of Ministers to member stated concerning the legal protection of persons suffering from mental

disorders placed as involuntary patients.

6. It considers that the time has come for the member states of the Council of Europe to adopt legal measures guaranteeing respect for human rights of psychiatric patients.

7. The Assembly therefore invites the Committee of Ministers to adopt a new recommendation based on the following rules:

(ⅰ) Admission procedure and conditions:

(a) compulsory admission must be resorted to in exceptional cases only and must comply with the following criteria:
  — there is a serious danger to the patient or to other persons;
  — an additional criterion could be that of the patient's treatment: if the absence of placement could lead to a deterioration or prevent the patient from receiving appropriate treatment;
(b) in the event of compulsory admission, the decision regarding placement in a psychiatric institution must be taken by a judge and the placement period must be specified. Provision must be made for the placement decision to be regularly and automatically reviewed. Principles established in the Council of Europe's forthcoming convention on bioethics must be respected in all cases;
(c) there must be legal provision for an appeal to be lodged against the decision;

(d) a code of patient's rights must be brought to the attention of patients on their arrival at a psychiatric institution;

(e) a code of ethics of psychiatrists should be drawn up inter alia on the basis of the Hawaii Declaration approved by the General Assembly of the World Psychiatric Association in Vienna in 1983.

(ii) Treatment:

(a) a distinction has to be made between handicapped and mentally ill patients;

(b) lobotomies and electroconvulsive therapy may not be performed unless informed written consent has been given by the patient or a person, counsellor or guardian, chosen by the patient as his or her representative and unless the decision has been confirmed by a select committee not composed exclusively of psychiatric experts;

(c) there must be an accurate and detailed recording of the treatment given to the patient;

(d) there must be adequate nursing staff appropriately trained in the care of such patients;

(e) patients must have free access to a "counsellor" who is independent of the institution; similarly, a "guardian" should be responsible for looking after the interests of minors;

(f) an inspection system similar to that of the European Committee for the Prevention of Torture and Inhuman or Degrading Treatment or Punishment should be set up.

(ⅲ) Problems and abuses in psychiatry:

(a) the code of ethics must explicitly stipulate that it is forbidden for therapists to make sexual advances to patients;

(b) the use of isolation cells should be strictly limited and accommodation in large dormitories should also be avoided;

(c) no mechanical restraint should be used. The use of pharmaceutical means of restraint must be proportionate to the objective sought, and there must be no permanent infringement of individuals' rights to procreate;

(d) scientific research in the field of mental health must not e undertaken without the patient's knowledge, or against his or her will or the will of his or her representative, and must be conducted only in the patient's interest.

(ⅳ) Situation of detained persons:

(a) any person who is imprisoned should be examined by a doctor;

(b) a psychiatrist and specially trained staff should be attached to each penal institution;

(c) the rules set out above and the rules of ethics should be applied to detained persons and, in particular, medical confidentiality should be maintained in so far as this is compatible with the demands of detention;

(d) sociotherapy programmes should be set up in certain penal institutions for detained persons suffering from personality disorders.

옮긴이 소개

신영전
서울대학교 보건대학원 박사
한양대학교 예방의학교실 부교수
국가인권위원회 정신장애인인권전문위원회 전문위원
번역 『사회역학』(한울, 2003)
　　『보건의료개혁의 정치학』(한울, 2005)
공저 『보건의료개혁의 새로운 모색』(한울, 2006)

최영은
서울대학교 보건대학원 석사
국립의료원 중앙응급의료센터 응급의료기술지원단 연구원

한울아카데미 962

정신장애인의 인권 향상을 위한 지침

ⓒ 신영전·최영은, 2007

지은이 | 세계보건기구 정신보건 및 약물남용예방 분과
옮긴이 | 신영전·최영은
펴낸이 | 김종수
펴낸곳 | 도서출판 한울

편집책임 | 이수동
편집 | 배은희

초판 1쇄 인쇄 | 2007년 7월 25일
초판 1쇄 발행 | 2007년 8월 6일

주소 | 413-832 파주시 교하읍 문발리 507-2(본사)
      121-801 서울시 마포구 공덕동 105-90 서울빌딩 3층(서울 사무소)
전화 | 영업 02-326-0095, 편집 02-336-6183
팩스 | 02-333-7543
홈페이지 | www.hanulbooks.co.kr
등록 | 1980년 3월 13일, 제406-2003-051호

Printed in Korea.
ISBN 978-89-460-3768-7 93330

* 책값은 겉표지에 있습니다.